WEEKS

BOOKS BY HANNAH WEINER

Clairvoyant Journal (Angel Hair, 1978)
Little Books/Indians (Roof, 1980)
Nijole's House (Potes & Poets Press, 1981)
The Code Poems (Open Studio, 1982)
Spoke (Sun & Moon, 1984)
Written In/The Zero One (Post Neo, 1985)
Weeks (Xexoxial, 1990)
The Fast (United Artists, 1992)
Silent Teachers / Remembered Sequel (Tender Buttons, 1993)
We Speak Silent (Roof, 1997).
PAGE (Roof, 2002)
Hannah Weiner's Open House (Kenning Editions, 2007)

weeks
hannah weiner

Photographs by Barbara Rosenthal

xexoxial editions west lima wisconsin 2008

These poems have appeared in the following publications: Cheap Review, Reality Studios, Pessimistic Labor, HOW(ever), Pome. Thanks to Ann Bogle & Allegra Wakest for their assistance with the 2nd edition.

1st edition 1990
2nd edition 2008
3rd edition 2010

Designed by mIEKAL aND. Back cover photograph by Richard Dillon.

©Hannah Weiner 1990
©Charles Bernstein 2008 in trust for Hannah Weiner
photographs ©Barbara Rosenthal 1990, 2008, 2010

ISBN 0-9770049-7-X
ISBN-13 978-0-9770049-7-3

Xexoxial Editions
10375 County Highway Alphabet
La Farge, WI 54639

perspicacity@xexoxial.org

www.xexoxial.org

By Charles Bernstein

Every day. Day by day. The hours hang and the headlines punctuate a passage through time that we move through, head bowed at the collision of flesh and indoctrination. Yet there might be (might there be?) some doctrine to get us out of this vicious circle of self-enclosing artifacts that we call news, as if the world was already lost before we could speak a word to it.

In Hannah Weiner's Weeks, the daily bite of world-event narrative achieves the grandeur, perhaps the quiet desperation, of background music (ambient ideology). Weeks is an unnerving foray in a world of prefabricated events: a world we seem to have fallen into, as if from the cradle.

Weeks was written in a small notebook, one page per day for fifty weeks. Each page of the book is the equivalent of a single week, with each day taking its toll in about five lines. The material, says Weiner, is all found – "taken at the beginning from written matter and TV news and later almost entirely from TV news."

Here parataxis (the serial juxtapositions of sentences) takes on an ominous tone in its refusal to draw connections. Weeks, in its extremity, represents the institutionalization of collage into a form of evenly hovering emptiness that actively resists analysis or puncturing. In Weeks, the virus of news is shown up as a pattern of reiteration and displacement, tale without a teller. Yet, while Weiner follows a strict poetic method of refusing the "lyrical interference of ego," the result is that these deanimated metonymies take on a teller, as if to call it "Hannah." This is the vortical twisting, or transformation, at the heart of Weeks' prosodic inquisition.

Weeks is poetic homeopathy: a weak dose of the virus to immunize our systems—let's say consciousnesses-against it.

What do we make of our everyday lives: make of them, make out of them? What do we make of, that is, these materials that we can no where (not anymore) avoid, avert our ears as we do, or, as in poetic practice, hide behind the suburban laws of laundered lyricism?

Weiner's Weeks is a shocking cul de sac to a tradition of the found in American poetry—a tradition that includes, by any brief accounting, Charles Reznikoff's Testimony, Sterling Brown's ethnographic encounters with the black oral tradition, William Burrough's cut-ups, Jack Spicer's "received" poems, Jackson MacLow's processing of source material, or Ronald Johnson's erasure of Milton in Radi Os; not to leave out Weiner's own Clairvoyant Journal, where what is found is the words seen (projected? transferred?) onto the objects and bodies surrounding her. Cul de sac not in the sense of "no more to be found," any more than no more to be lost. Only that in the world of Weeks there's no way out and ascent upward is effectively blocked, since Weeks presents a world in which "I went by [can only go by] the information I received," i.e., not very far. What's left is to descend into this world of "our" very own making, to attend (to) its forms so better to reckon with it. "The standoff began as a botched robbery."

weeks 1-50

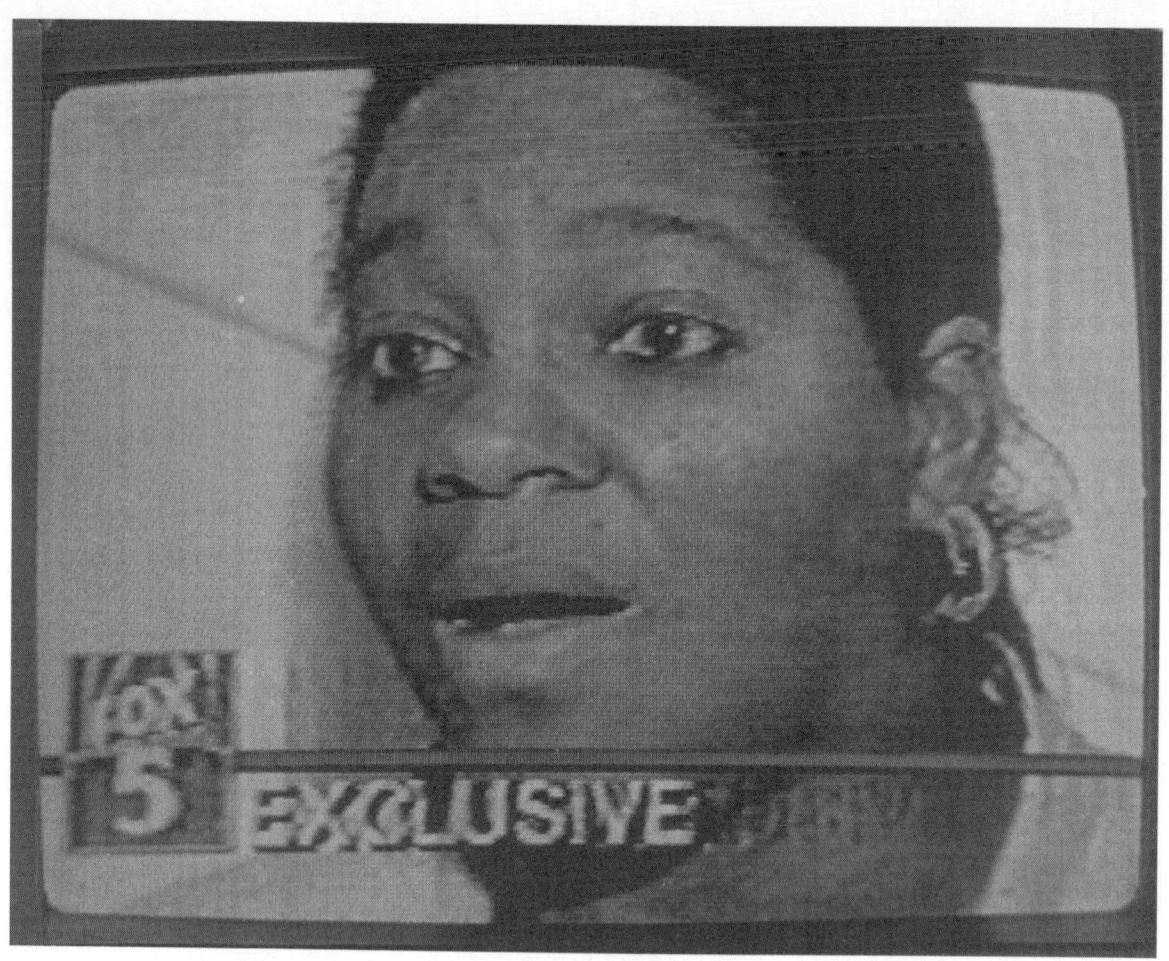

One idea leads to another   One line before the day   Hardly any money was raised   Another idea leads to this eating chicken at Bernadette's   Eating nuts at my house   You don't have to read the newspaper on Guatemala but it sits on the table   It doesn't create life   A stitch in time   The page is written in for me I did it my self at another time   In the spirit of creation everyone is too loud   There is never a reason for everything the ten best movies of the year   In time on time   They're upstairs making a decision that could save a man's life   The death of Carl in case the heart doesn't fit him   One inmate was killed by his fellow prisoners   I'm too bored to talk to you   I didn't know Carl I have my own deaths to remember   The better the butter the bitter the writer   More news to follow   Pavarotti plus   The image of pop corn   So you could see just what a year on film it was There is no pleasure in starting at the top of a blank page they are having a wedding   She likes the end papers but not the book   Carrying the coffeepot on the tray requires two hands incompetent was one of the Crimson's swearwords   She spent more and more time in bed waiting for sleep and for dreams   She wrote one page a day in this journal   Answers to 700 questions about the Boston rock scene   Looking to the past for their lost ideas I didn't want to tear everything down and start again   The folding bed belonged to the poet Swinburne   An answer to a prayer an unbeatable combination   A nice sunshiny day   I can bring to it the same passion and intensity that I thought, for years, I could only bring to the study of Russian history   An off again on again countdown   We have main engine start   It is appropriate to start at the top of the page   Today is the day to water the plant   Harvard prepares to celebrate the 350th anniversary of its founding   The Poetry Project's grant from the National Endowment was cut from 50,000 to 20,000   A Handwritten Modern Classic is difficult to read.

WEEKS 1

WEEKS 2

Sips of morning coffee alternate with bits of crackers and jam   Film Forum announces an evening with Yevgeny Yevtushenko   Concerts of sixteenth century music for lute don't happen often   The yahrtzeit for my Aunt Reka is Shevat 3, next Monday   Dial the weather for the temperature   I have just finished reading Harvard Magazine   On the way to the Dr. to get a shot   Residential Continuing Care Retirement Community for those who wish to live life to its fullest   Limousine and driver, cook, housekeeping, baby sitter, tour guide   Breakfast is over   A long letter from Pete Spence from Oct or Nov is on the table   So are the books he sent, Quilt, Some-one, Skywriter, and Handwritten Modern Classic and some promo material from Sybella, a cooperative press in Australia   A new law bans mandatory retirement   I ate eleven crackers to average out with yesterday's thirteen   Today is the day to wash my hair   Writing that goes beyond traditional ideas   political arena moves to the streets   I rarely invent anything to say   Boustrophedon (bústrofídan) as the ox turns in plowing—refers to writing from left to right and then reversing direction to continue writing now right to left   Yes, the window installation process is a pain in the _____   Reading the owner's newsletter 1986 budget shows no increase in maintenance   What is man, or the son of man, What is man, O lord, what is man O Lord, what is man that Thou takest knowledge of him?   Or the son of man that thou doest regard him?   Man is like unto a breath; His days are as a shadow that passes away   O Heavenly Father, remember the soul of my beloved aunt who has gone to her eternal home to be reunited with Thee   O may her soul be bound up in the bond of life, a living blessing in our midst   Amen   Dear Aunt, I recall the many hours we spent together in happy fellowship   I shall ever hold sacred the memory of your love and loyalty

May God grant that the recollections of your life stimulate me to noble thinking and righteous living   O Lord, I put my trust in thee who art the source of all life and my strength in sorrow   Amen   He's up to the minute and doesn't know what to do next   A blank day   The TV broke   Breakfast at six   If evolution has moved along a linear path of progress   Wild America is our campus   I'm married and I have a sixteen month old baby boy   Kiss me you fool   One thousand seven hundred and twenty dollars   The day is over   Females try to mate with the dominate male, which will later extend protection to infants he had sired   89.9 for labor plus parts   A caracara, or carrion eater   One fieldworker, Brent Houston, personally spotted more than eighty animals   Why not take some into captivity   Would we have gotten to the numbers if we had to write it   Does writing take more or less energy than talking   You have a habit of dealing with all disagreements with me by walking out or not talking   A silence that was engendered by hostility   Importance of gestures to convey emotions (expressions on face)   Comedy element of silence   Rigidity element of silence   Effect of silence on raising energy from any one chakra to another   Venus left the morning sky in January, and this month Jupiter enters it   Is 4:30 too late to be of any help   Martin Luther King Jr.'s birthday   One thing that links them all together—another female agent was killed then   She knew the risk they all did   When all else fails create a diversion   I can get a drunken driver off the street   If you side with us you side with justice, you side with righteousness, you side with peace   I have a dream maybe out of this whole business there might be some changes that will come   Right now we are sitting in the main square of Merida enjoying the passing people (who are also watching us)

WEEKS 3

WEEKS 4

She's grateful to her new boyfriend for a new lease on life   Many other cities broke the record high for the day   It's a woman's political issue   It is absolutely the woman's right to decide whether she will or whether she will not have an abortion 13 years after abortion was legalized   Friday and Saturday prying into the private lives of public people   Questions about any relationship between the two   The US Mediterranean fleet   The US insists Sidra is international waters   Italy today issued an international arrest warrant   The opposition challenging his election   Just how long is a day on Uranus   Higher pulse rates, necessary for building fitness, seem easier because more muscles share the exercise   Wildly independent and beloved of the younger set   The white minority government   There's a lot for other cats to live up to   Including nine thin rings which are barely visible   It discovered active volcanoes on undiscovered moons   The Ball Court seen from the Jaguar's Temple, Chichen Itza   If mankind is guided by such radiation, ianstead of being destroyed by that of atomic fission, all will enjoy eternal peace in the world   A man like that would be unhappy in heaven   I am innocent of these changes   The church fully understands   Jewish concern   walking westward in the city   I just try to refine the boy's talents a bit   I have reason to believe that someone is trying to poison her to death   Interest rates go down   Admission to Museum field station in Arizona   There will be Several city employees indicted   Travel opportunities led by Museum Scientists to all parts of the world   They voted over the weekend to accept a new contract   I think there'll be some snow   Below 0 in 21 states   Challenger explodes   The tragedy defies any easy explanation   There were no signs of abnormalities on the screen   The twin solid boosters had not shown any trouble at all   The huge ball of fire shortly after 11:30 this morning   A minute and ten seconds into the flight—a fireball   Never a disaster like this in the history of the space program

America's space program went up in flames yesterday as the world watched in horror   Yesterday a nation in shock today mourning and a search for answers   What blew up that ship   They are gathering paltry pieces of debris from the ocean   They consider one piece 12 inches long a find   The computers did not detect anything wrong at all   The officials here are not speculating at all   People watched it happen from their balconies and backyards   Some of the debris is washing up on shore   The teacher turned astronaut   I was very upset and felt bad for the family   They were married for 18 years   Every piece we pick out of the water hurts a little   The boosters were destroyed on purpose   Why were those vapors, the flames, there   There may never be a complete answer   Mid day memorial service for the seven who died   This greenish debris contains hazardous materials   This house where she lived with her husband and children   We bid you goodbye we will never forget you   New stars in the divided sky   From a treaty   The interview lists, with the references, they're all set   Mission Impossible doesn't explain everything   It is not the critic who counts   The blow torch theory   It may indicate a hole in the booster rocket   A rainforest symposium was held   The destruction of these forests has become a critical problem   Resistance to these colonial forms has been strongest among the Moro peoples of the south and the Cordillera peoples of the North   After you build the dams, where do we hang the light bulbs   Are you trying to sell me a ticket to breathe   In the three years which followed, more than 300 AIM members and supporters were shot; of these approximately 70 are known to have died   He is also the individual who threatened Anna Mae Aquash with death prior to her execution-style slaying in 1975   By 1976, with the AIM leadership in exile or facing interminable trials and with the organization's ranks thoroughly decimated, the FBI dismantled much of its Rapid City effort   Was assigned to the Rapid City field office once again in 1982, during the height of the AIM confrontation with federal authorities concerning the occupation of Yellow Thunder Camp in the Black Hills...a sign that the possibility was there

WEEKS 5

WEEKS 6

Allah is the light of the heavens and of the earth   The light of Wakan-Tanka is upon my people   God is the sun beaming light everywhere   Following the light, the sage takes care of all   The Lord is my light; who shall I fear   The radiance of Buddha shines ceaselessly ARTSCAPE is a stiff, city-manipulated instance of institutionalized provincialism   People party but do not reach for their checkbooks   The difference between Baltimore and New Orleans is the difference between imitation-Socialism and imitation-Capitalism   Were has seriousness gone   By 9^{am} the George Washington had no problem   I thought it brought good luck to me, I wouldn't ever have to use it   Only minor delays   62 people have been killed in election related violence   Election day chaos in the Philippines   The president for 20 years is in a fight for his life   It was a day for mad celebration in Haiti   Today the army emerged as the nation's savior   Their wedding cost 3 million dollars   Also called President for life but his term ran out this morning   Close vote count in the Philippines   Voters sat on ballot boxes to prevent their being switched   Reports of stuffed ballot boxes in neat almost similar handwriting   Instances of fraud   Like the last time they swapped spies here   We've never had anything on this scale   Built to protest the college's 63 million dollar investment in South Africa   Still her death came as a shock   Votes were being manipulated   He saw massive fraud by Marcos   The year of the Tiger   Government officials if scientists in this country   Liquor isn't all that has health officials worried   I'd like to read your story when you've finished it   Oh sure, now I remember you   Do you ever get a little jealous   You really don't want to be doing this, do you   Was it worth it?   Every penny   Rolls, wingovers, split esses and Immelman turns   Move the transmitter gently   Do not over-control   Taxi, take-off, land   If the glide is too steep, flatten it with some up-elevator   You'll be ready for pretty takes a walk into freedom   Crossed the bridge from east to west

Building staff members have the right to perform services for Building residents if specifically requested and expect compensation therefore while off duty, though may not advertise the availability of such services in the Building   Complaints regarding the service of the Building shall be made in writing   We have behavioral medical specialists   I met an at home coordinator   The teachers really care about if you pass   It's time to stand up and cheer for the doer   Six protesters were arrested outside the plant today   Don't you think I should call the plumber   I want the name and address of the man   Both forms of the insect produce the brilliant red dye, but the domestic form, generally preferred because it is larger, is the only one that is commercially available   Our research boys have engineered a scientific breakthrough   I've made up my mind and I want out   We're looking for bigger and better things   You're a lucky man   Convinced she would crack the walls   of prejudice   The roof of this house was too low for her   She had to stay at the homes of friends because no hotel would accept her   The nation's black stars had made remarkable inroads   Everybody's in on the conspiracy   I would leave out the men's room attendant   Acting is like an exploration of the soul   I think you're pretty lucky I came along   You need a set of perspectives if you kill yourself   They make sure you pay for the sessions you miss   She tells us you've been seeing a psychiatrist   I know how you feel—we'll go inside and talk   First you doubt, then you assume, then you question, then you prove   I hope that it will encourage others   It's no use, I've done that already   A big decision is made by the makers of Tylenol   Sue the company sooner or later   They were more concerned about the consumers than they were about the company   It was a theory   The Philippine peso suffered its worst devaluation in fifteen years   Human error appears to have been the cause   A victory for bad politics   The engineering decisions were over-ridden

WEEKS 8

Charges both men with racketeering and conspiracy   Free of the clubhouse types   As the days fold into weeks   We assume that everyone is a darn crook   Russell Means got shrapnel wounds in his belly in Nicaragua   Bill Means is going to Geneva   Conditions of life for Spanish women prior to 1936 were oppressive and repressive in the extreme   Flooding has long been a problem   It denied shooting down a passenger plane   I like you to come down hard on caution   Did you know that some foreign wines could be hazardous to your health   Stopped that bad habit a long time ago   Now wouldn't you say that someone out there has a pretty bad conscience   Forgetting things we'd worked on for days   So dedicated he tired me out   Leonard Crow Dog calls saying there's the thirteenth anniversary of Wounded Knee   George Tisch asks me to read in Detroit   The only things that are guaranteed in life are death and taxes   I mentioned this whole notion of keeping very accurate records   Now you can freeze your own blood for future use   You really don't know who you're reaching   I think it makes it a little bit easier for them to grow old gracefully   The new record holder   That works out to 60¢ per square foot   Why would anyone do it   He has pled not guilty   Well I was seated in a chair right over there   I will increase that tuition commitment   The corruption goes from the very top to the very bottom   He fled the country but the government seized his house   Men have to buy or rent their jobs   They feel distressed and dismayed   We are going to put in additional protection   A peaceful transition to a new government   I intend also to protect my life   Is there any peaceful way out in Manila   The preservation of a stable ally   Then I'm afraid we're all going to have to lose our patience   Eastern sells its airline   And the great will to do something for the Philippine people   Although denying him asylum we supplied the airforce plane that carried him to France   Transition has been all things considered remarkably clear   They were struck head on by another car   There was too much pressure to keep the launch on schedule

Theories have to be supported by facts   About 6 minutes or more late   Over half the fleet will be clean and graffiti free
They unanimously opposed the launch on that cold Tuesday morning   The former president has landed in Hawaii   The mood in Manila is one of hope   Some art treasures appear to have been moved already   Impalpable and enslaving, like a charm, like a whispered promise of mysterious delight   He was fascinated by the duality of the jungle, that everything is growing and decaying simultaneously   Olmeyer was the son-in-law of a sea-captain and trader, Captain Lingard, whose wealth came from the river   Fly to Boston for the wedding   Oh boy, do I hope I'm wrong   Did you really expect to find anything   You always were a sucker for that combination   It's quite an act you've been putting on   I knew that he would never agree   Sorry I crashed the party   Today Amy and Jordan get married   Registration forms are available at any local office   Yes, sweetheart I'm trying to find my sister   Now get right over there   You're an angel   You're too slick for your own good   The schoolgirl manner, blushing, stammering   It was all in the spirit of the piece   All right everybody let's go on with the rehearsal   Travel back from Boston on the 2 o'clock shuttle   Sure I got ambition   You'd like that wouldn't you   Will Corazon Aquino declare a revolutionary government   That five bucks extra for the waterbed   This is not too bad, is it   Sounds of laughter   An explosion in the whirlpool bath   They're setting up a scholarship in his name   No one told the astronauts about trouble with the rocker booster seals   Was there undue pressure   There is no great clamor in the country for aid for the Contras   There's indications that it's owned by corporations   There are a couple of embarrassing political problems   Just after Palme was shot last Friday the manhole blew up   Mouth to muzzle resuscitation   They use young people as watchers   A total file on the assassination of John F Kennedy has been released

WEEKS 10

We get along wonderfully   It was something that inspired me   Examining baby food jars for glass   I can read I can drive   How to better cope with the loss of your pet   Americans own over 150 million pets   Replacing the pet with another one to love can really be a good thing to do   Hoping to be the best speller of the lot   Will you tell him   I'm sorry, really sorry   I had nothing to do with it   It's just that we'd like to see you stay in one piece   He's taking it pretty hard   As we all know, no news is good news   One of the two O rings may have been the wrong diameter   Dealing with parts that had to fit precisely together   Georgia O'Keefe died at 98   Imagine for a moment that tomorrow morning every volunteer in this country decided to quit working   I know they're supposed to be charming but they always remind me of the laundromat   But we are going to need a bit more   Most people are sincere   Everybody who comes to know them comes to know that   To think is not to put anything down   It's too cute, it just doesn't say enough   Then something happened, or didn't happen   Today everything kept coming back wrong   Is it always the middle of the night when you think about time   Women's involvement in the Community Service, Elderly Affairs, Women's Issues, Education and Environmental Action committees has been consistently and significantly higher than men's   Enthusiasm is the greatest asset in the world   It beats money and power and influence   No one ever regarded the first of January with indifference   Subsequent dives provided positive identification of Challenger crew compartment debris and the existence of crew remains   Catholic principles and concepts of Catholic medical practice would be violated and there is no way we could continue together   In stories told to children and in sermons delivered to adults, Maimonides was extolled   Ray Milland, dead of cancer at 81   This is woman's history month   It's important to me   I don't get your train of thought   I haven't worked that out yet   A vote against the president is a vote for communism   Thousands demonstrating in the streets   Endorsed free elections soon

For several years, the press printed only the official story
of army-URNG confrontations under the threat of government
censorship   Today, the URNG actions are too big for the press
to ignore despite continuing government threats   they also
threatened Nicaraguan President Daniel Ortega if he visited
Guatemala for the inauguration   Don't you know, black is
beautiful   An alleged co-ed sex ring in a carriage house
Obviously those weapons are weapons of intimidation   One
policeman on drugs is one too many   He was never an active suspect
Recovered more body parts from the flight deck area   On Civil
Defense Patrols: Cerezo says he will make these voluntary, and
put departmental committees now controlled by the military in
civilian hands   Listen, I don't understand your treatment
He plunged a knife into his heart   He was pronounced dead at
11 o'clock   I don't know where they get the strength
Open the mind to everything, and then follow the ink   One
suitable phrase leaves no hope   Why are there places where
some thing is not happening   The president was taking his own
shots at the Nicaraguan government   The Soviets dismissed
the invitation as propaganda   Neither of us is satisfied
A grieving widow says a final goodbye   All the good things
that he did for Queen's County   We have a system that boasts
of presuming innocence   As many as a million spectators are
expected   With Fifth Avenue to look forward to tomorrow
There are still hostages in Lebanon   The complaints about
the ribbons are a way of renewing interest   St. Patrick's Day
so you would unhook the respirator   Domestic violence is taking
place in almost every corner of the country   All officers must
take the training   900 parts any one of which could jeopardize
a space flight if it failed   If the fear stops you from what
you have to do   A chemical imbalance   Your arguments with him
may be political   A royal no comment   Does it look like they
have the votes this time   It's a shame you found it so quickly
All you have to do is press the right button   Keep on walking
and you shall be free   This time we are fully prepared to act

WEEKS 12

What about the company that dumped this stuff   The whole town is now endangered   Gay rights is a concept not easily accepted   His conscience or his political career   Investigators have seized the records of two cab companies   The debate continued today with no let up   You're sure   Thank you   He could tie a lot of loose ends together   If you need anything, just let me know   We're living in freedom   I started to dress for Spring today and I wound up in wool   Looks like a stroke of luck to me   Would we know one if we found one   Lewis came here from Poland in his 20s   He's 100 years old   After traces of rat poison were found   It began with a series of telephone threats   The rupture of one joint is to blame   We're very much interested in that theory   Panama said no their request for asylum   The free and open exchange of information and ideas is essential to an academic community   The number of vent "regular" reached six or seven at times last year and drinking, which is not permitted at Cambridge shelters for the homeless, was also a problem   Brutality and foul play should receive the same summary punishment as a man who cheats at cards   When was the catcher's mask invented   Harvard teams tend to have a higher quotient of individualists   I don't want to condone what she's doing   Private dealers don't talk about their profits   His equipment has been in action around the world   No identifying features   That's the point of impact   I'm sorry but it happens to be common knowledge   The official word is no comment   They have sunk the ship   The Soviet technicians are there   That was sufficient cause for the US to retaliate   This attack was entirely unprovoked   We deny Libya's claim   You don't reform apartheid, you destroy it   He still believed in non-violence   The proportion interested in careers in the arts is 7 percent—a ten-year high   They're calling for a Holy War   All is quiet off the coast of Libya   The purpose is to assert an international right   We don't belong in that part of the world

What is the extent of your participation   We made you a promise
and we're going to keep it   He quit when the pay-off scandal
in his department was made public   We expect further charges
A number of US outposts are sitting ducks   I think he poses
a real threat   It's not even allowed on buses or trains
This could have all sorts of legal and financial ramifications
I don't find that so incredible   There were still more
indictments today   How did you try to enact some change in the
community   Taking water samples along the river   Today is Good
Friday   I certainly wouldn't want to bring someone back to my
home who I wasn't thoroughly familiar with   Why would he make
those charges if there wasn't some kind of credibility to them
We don't want to have the public sour on the Democratic Party
If we survive the bellicosity and fiscal madness of these later
years of the twentieth century and have the chance to look back
from the first moments of the twenty-first century, we might
find in the decades just past a series of major transitions
in the course of science and human affairs   Today is Easter
Went to the East River Drive Park with Noa and Joss and
watched Joss play soccer   Kicked the ball home   Had tea
and chocolate cookies, organic wine and baked potato and went with
Noa to Theater 80 to see "Of Human Bondage" and "Rain"   As
any fool can tell they do have the ability to make people laugh
15% of the stock of Fiat is owned by the Libyan government
Air plane crashes in Mexico   Several brush fires are burning
out of control in New Jersey   Officials say it's the hot dry
weather   It's not our obligation to find that out   Kinda
scared when you live this close to them   The fires happen every
spring   Funeral services for James Cagney were held today   He
was 86 years old   I do not believe I'm the target of any in-
vestigation   There's a scandal in camel hair   The landing
gear collapsed   The price of oil dips below $10 a barrel

WEEKS 13

WEEKS 14

The explosion was supposed to be caused by a bomb in the luggage   They do have courage   The lure of the continent is still compelling   It's a common failing throughout the world   For now I must pass the rope and pic to another climber   Only 12% of the shuttle has been recovered   I despise these cowardly acts   Striking flight attendants were urging passengers to stay away   It's against the law to make false statements about having bombs once you're aboard an airline   They are looking at high tech waves to find out explosives   So where is everybody going on vacation this summer   He just couldn't adjust to his new state   The gunman is described as depressed and remorseful   Our generation is leaving the next a legacy of deficits, economic and ecological   It really is scary   Her mother defected to the West in 1967   He may have scared them off forever with his original plan to demolish the whole block   If children constituted a nation it would be the world's largest   Once fertile fields in Ethiopia's highlands may be abandoned in the next decade, although the land has been under continuous cultivation for many centuries   The Italians produce more wine than anyone else   A few scoundrels are ruining us all   Sales have tripled in ten years   A terrorist bomb ripped through a West Berlin discotheque   If you don't feel right about somebody just say no and walk away from them   It's like a direct attack on our religion   We're going to make a couple of grants today   This really is a school of hard knocks   In actuality the present government does not plan to bring about a deep transformation of Guatemalan society   A trustee's discretionary right to spend trust income for children's education and living requirements takes a detailed knowledge of the children and their needs   It takes away the craving for cocaine   What kind of financial problems have you been facing   Now we have independent committees around the country and there is a lot of activism of all types   There isn't the need for AIM to go around the country

Time is running out and I need some answers   Recently our Building lost one of its leading citizens, Miss Bea Kinn, who lived in apt 13c since our Building first opened   They say you were involved with this thing, the S.S.   We won't forget about you if you've committed murder, mass murder, or terrorism   Test them all before you sell them   This is the 100th day of this year   US ships are steaming toward Libya   But how far Cerezo will go in opposing Reagan's regional policy remains to be seen   The bruised and battered body of Beatriz Eugenia Barrios was found 2 days after the Dec 8 presidential election   The tenants barricaded themselves inside   I think we can keep it going almost indefinitely and so can Libya   We on the Board are planning to make extensive, necessary and long overdue repairs and replacements to the Building's roof, façade and exterior wall   The blue wall of silence   Spur of the moment—I'm impulsive myself   Don't worry I've got the 20 grand   I know kidnapping is a federal offense but what other choice do I have   Everybody makes mistakes   I am so tired of talking, aren't you   And then I'll thank you for it afterward   No one takes the thought of a major chemical leak lightly   He has not come clean about his days in the German army   They made such statements apparently to save their skins   You have yourself to blame because you were not more candid   How they use their money, funding cultural institutions   Hopefully it was an isolated case   The common market nations urged restraint on all sides   NASA hopes that this will provide the crucial clue about the rocket booster's leak   There's a great deal of voter apathy   Simone de Beauvoir died today at 78   They oppose the plant calling it environmentally unsound   Planes strike at Libya   There is a price to engaging in terrorism around the world   One F111 unaccounted for   I don't think it's going to achieve as much as the administration hoped for   Among the dead, the baby daughter of Qadaffi   Libya launches two missiles at a Coast Guard Station in Italy   We chose the ones we could identify the easiest

WEEKS 16

We've seen him stand up   He's alive, he's well and he's inside Libya   Do you think we can get out of this without the overriding support of our allies   I'm not ready for my life to end now, I'm a little scared about that   I would say the rules are changing in Libya   So what are you going to be doing about Saturday night   Then and only then can you put grace and beauty into what you do   Three Britons killed, one kidnapped   The pictures show vividly what the pilot and bombardier were after after   Unless we get rainfall we'll have difficulty getting through the drier season   An American is killed as terrorists retaliate   Reagan is a killer of children   There is no regulation, it's free enterprise   Have these young students learn something they couldn't have learned before   In Paterson it's gotten quite serious   Does the battle leave the room for a fourth daily paper   Except, of course, their need to be free   In Milan 15,000 marched in protest   I'm not some smart politician   One trailer was blown 1/4 mile   Remains of all seven astronauts have been recovered.   It's the first time he's played in his homeland in 61 years   You get some strong guys and ask them to be careful   He likes a good quality tone   The destruction was spread over a wide area   The newsmen see only what they are allowed to see   The overlap is not surprising, given thirty years of army rule, and underscores the powerful influence the military continues to exercise in every aspect of Guatemalan life   We don't like the standards any more than they do   We've been trying to get the government to tighten them   Now the children can have what they've always dreamed of, as well as us   Vicious tornadoes almost wiped out a whole town   Recovery operations for the shuttle's debris are winding down   It's sort of a nightmare version of the dating game   A piece of matzoh is not any old cracker   21 Libyans are behind bars in England   A record 12% decrease in the cost of gasoline   Only if Ryan White isn't there   The Israeli government says it has no involvement or knowledge of the deal

He wants a new agenda for New York   That won't be necessary, thanks   She was well aware of my concern over wild-life   He counted on America to be passive   A nation-wide crackdown on pornography   They are not linked to the I.R.A.   Not all terrorism is state sponsored   It's the court of last resort for the little guy who's been ripped off   Collecting the money you've won is the tough part   You are one of a hundred with a chance to go   The Crying Baby Clinic   I let her put herself back to sleep   Parts of the Challenger were still being recovered from the Atlantic   We wore our rigs under our coats as we took the elevator to the 86th floor   We just waited for a red light   It's a chance to prove that with planning you can do most anything   A court order kept the schools open   Here's a man who has lied about a very important point in history   The precautions in Tokyo promise to be more elaborate than ever   His government is paying up to be prepared   ... and the Puerto Rican government on tax matters   They had best be prepared for the consequence   Most development aid assumes that boosting Third World economics will translate into other basic gains such as improved health, nutrition, education, and a falling birth rate   I am especially pleased to run for reelection to the Board of Directors, now that the first year of our co-op has been completed   I hope that you will read the enclosed booklet and study the background information and statements of the candidates   Dudley is an avid fisherman who says he fishes waters throughout the world as an excuse to travel to remote places   How close we came to catastrophe there   The lack of good hard solid information   Are those two rights on a collision course these days   I don't believe you're improving the quality of the information supplied   Are the lights shining brighter on the greater white way

WEEKS 17

WEEKS 18

This is invisible stuff up there   Folks were just lying around on the grass   This year we have carefully added new titles not previously available to a national audience as well as selecting titles from last year's list of publishers   Does a healthy body mean a healthy mind   The Soviets have vastly understated their losses   We've got nuclear trucking going through our city   Ham radio is always used in the initial stages of a disaster   There is fear of loss of face and world opinion and the space program will go on   We're here on 67th St and Lexington Ave.   That international aid be allowed into the Ukraine   An expert on bone marrow transplant   Perhaps he will offer them access to the American list   The documents were found in the national archive in Washington   A resistance to the hiring of gays on the part of the membership   How do we know some of those haven't infiltrated the police dept.   They're disgracing the job   The crunch comes when the issue goes public   U.S. oil companies or their subsidiaries still pump most of Libya's oil   Radiation clouds dissipating   It was a special day for some special dogs   We'll brighten up your patio, shove a couple of creepers up your trellis   This was Haiti last February   No charge against the former first lady seems too extreme   Nice weather, spring, it's so wonderful   Do you know the name of the astronaut who became America's first man in space   It happened today twenty-five years ago   Will the 49,000 who had to be evacuated from the area ever be able to go home again   That's something I can't give any credence to without a professional evaluation   A mother and her 13 year old son were both selling drugs   This is holocaust remembrance day   How big a ransom did the letter ask for

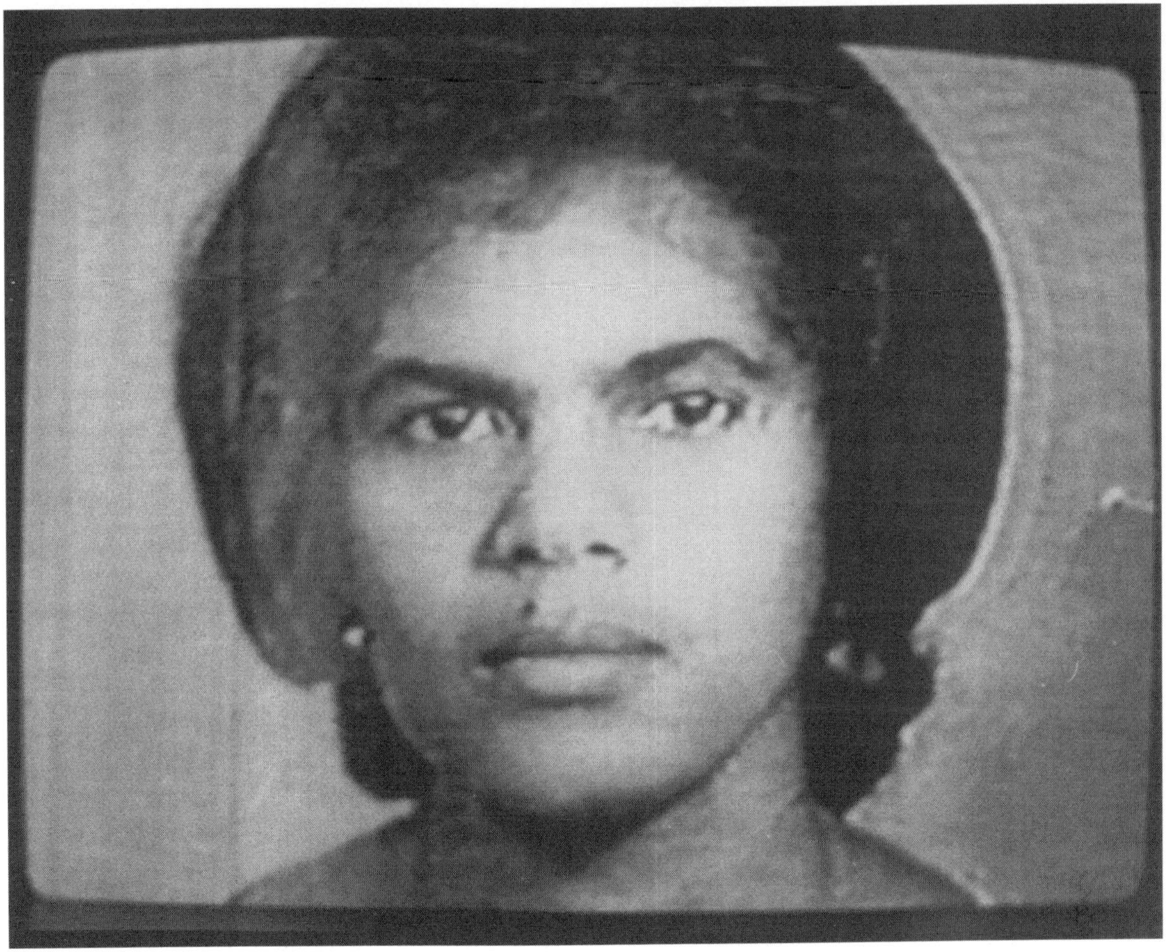

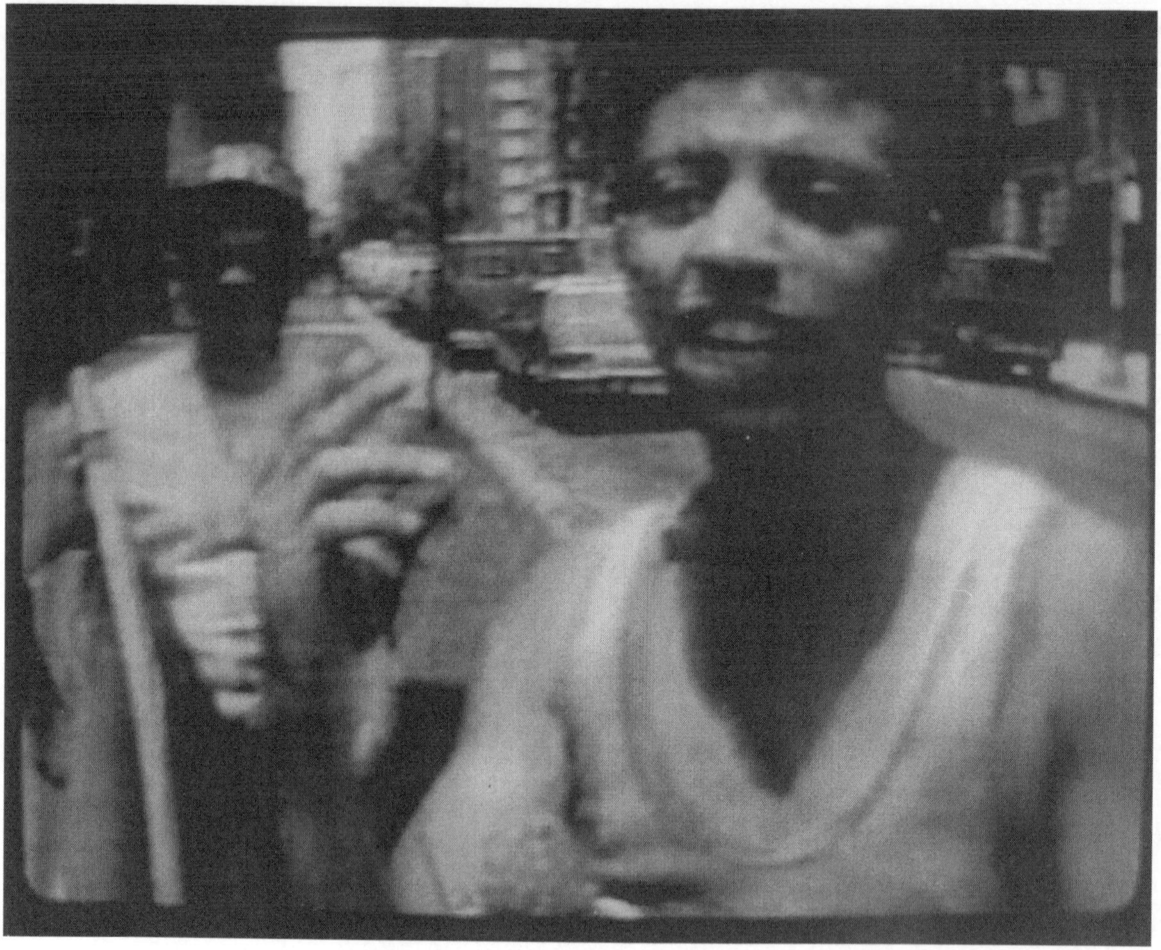

You cannot see the laser beam but you can see the results   He insists he'll be found innocent when he goes on trial next fall   But for the oldest of our city's immigrants the dream was long ago and far away   But as times change so do immigrant communities   The roof of a second reactor evidently did catch fire   It has to be smothered and that may take several weeks   We don't want food irradiation in NYC   The defendants deny any wrong doing   The police believe the killer knew the woman and the wooded area   The fire in the reactor appears to be out   The Soviet harvest of wheat is expected to be 5-10% short   I think the problem now is water contamination   The senate acted in a very radical way   It was rainy out and the street was slick at the time of the accident   That burger you had for lunch may give you more than indigestion   You get two games for one buck but you gotta be in it to win it   Coney Island Hospital is being evacuated because of a fire in a generator   An army colonel is accused of murder and torture in Haiti   The city is a much more attractive place to make an investment   He knows as much about lie detectors as anyone   Nervousness has absolutely nothing to do with the examination   Richard Nixon, probably the most dishonest man I ever met   I don't agree with some of the decisions he made in the Supreme Court but he had the guts to make them   At the present time we are running more units than we normally run on a Monday   I feel very bad that he's not around here to give his side of the story   One plant worker was expelled from the Communist Party   Fletcher predicted it won't be long before we're flying again   In my opinion the aforementioned financial statements present fairly the financial position as of December 31, 1985, and the results of its operation for the period then ended in conformity with generally accepted accounting principles   A warning to stay away from certain imported foods

WEEKS 20

She's a latchkey youngster, home alone after school   The Yonkers school board asked for four years to integrate, but that was turned down   I will review whatever options exist   We have to continually offer something new   It's a two-fold issue, jobs, housing and crime   The job is 40 days ahead of schedule   The complications may not be worth the risk   The problem of dental implants all along is to find material to bond with the bone   If you want to get a good night's sleep it is suggested you hold your baby more during the day   If you don't act please think of all the people you'll be writing off   A dramatic rescue on a frozen Oregon mountain   They saved each other with their respective body heat   Emphasize the uniqueness of each of them   It costs $95,000 to raise a child to age 18   Most of the buildings on her block are being rehabilitated   The recent news bulletin of the Council on Hemispheric Affairs states that in the three months since Cerizo's inauguration in January, there have been over 100 assassinations and 40 disappearances   Ivan, their youngest, now works at the prevention center   The kids want to have fun, and to their surprise, they do   How the city coped with a million extra people   There are obviously a lot of wise drivers in the metropolitan area   There was innocent touching without abuse   They decided not to buy anything in the white business district   He should not have had his bail revoked   His memory had changed because he had been intimidated   No charges have been filed against the bus driver   She wasn't hurt because she was wearing her seat belt   He is charged with breaking the law he has sworn to uphold   Morning commuters   Still faced spotlights run on emergency generators   My fingers are crossed but we're working hard   Today the Bronx is being rebuilt   I'm very sad to leave the department after thirty and a half years   Students play a vital role   The first question they ask is does it hurt

Rushing to do repairs the housing court had ordered   The worst kinds of conditions, almost concentration camps   He was trained and funded by Syria   Many Americans will not travel abroad this year   Plastic guns are the latest in high-tech fire power   Would you spell out a little more clearly what you think the FBI man was trying to do   Union officials said today it was not even close   Today the New York Public Library celebrated its 75th birthday   That cuts the survival rate by 50%   I think I'm very down to earth   Demonstrators were reported to have looted some market stalls in the city of Chiquimula and to have attempted to set fire to the marketplace in Zacapa   Debris was scattered for at least a 100 yards in all directions   The other alternative is stay at the beach all summer, just don't come back   Congress had curtailed military aid to Guatemala in 1977 on human-rights grounds, but the Reagan Administration argued that the new government of General Efrain Rios Montt was improving conditions dramatically   The Administration was requesting only a modest appropriation to buy spare parts for three army helicopters   But people were holding hands, carrying on as far away as Alaska   There may be as many as 21 million hungry Americans   None of those reports could be confirmed   He also served as ambassador to India   To breathe life into a dead economy   No spectators were injured   Runners pounding the pavement to help famine in Africa   The ceremony stretched from the Atlantic to the Pacific   This woman's brother is missing in action   As quickly as the police leave, the drag racers return   Their aim is 50 million dollars to feed and house the homeless   It sounds like it's just packed with ingredients to please an audience   Each order must earn its own keep   The retirement picture does not look good   It's designed for the entire family   Strong abdominal muscles help you avoid lower back pain   I'm quite some guy, I tell you   Are you intimidated by marrying the Kennedy clan   Two workers are dead and an industrial complex is leveled by fire

WEEKS 22

Now this whole Coney Island is out of order   Speech discourteous to the public   It begins with checking doctors' competency every few years   If she's lucky she may only have to pay a substantial fine   Critics say the report goes far beyond just education   Troublesome delays for many days ahead   After they beat him they didn't have to stab him   They were protesting the use of non-union labor on that site   They hope they never have to find out how it feels to be in a company town when the company closes up shop   59 people remain in serious condition   The baby was absolutely clean, no trace of radiation whatever   Despite illness, his collection of May 8 was a triumph   A fight over a girl that turned violent   Should drugs be used to treat depression   The talking treatment is as good as pills   May 30th, 1431, Joan of Arc was burned at the stake   A few successful films will make all the difference   Mass Transit Systems Corporation of Philadelphia has been supplying the Guatemalan government with laser-aimed rifle sights "for several years" according to the company president   The beach is enforcing its ban on beer   I ran the course several times, both directions   When the weather is cool and not hot, there's plenty of water   The blast ripped a hole in the street under a parked van   The 40th annual Tony Awards   Who's to blame for the city budget   The annual Puerto Rican Day Parade swept up Fifth Avenue   We're making a big impact on the community   The Red Sox still lead the American League East   We don't believe warnings will suffice   Why after all them trees have been there 27 years   I am totally committed to the cause of black activism   Staten Island—some call it the forgotten borough, some call it the racist borough   We don't use contraception as well as we should   The stroke of luck that saved his life was an apple tree that broke his fall   It only costs $10 and any superintendent or handyman could install it   It now takes 30 seconds to reach an operator compared to the usual 2 seconds   Yep, some downright fancy roping saved the day   This was grand, it was presidential

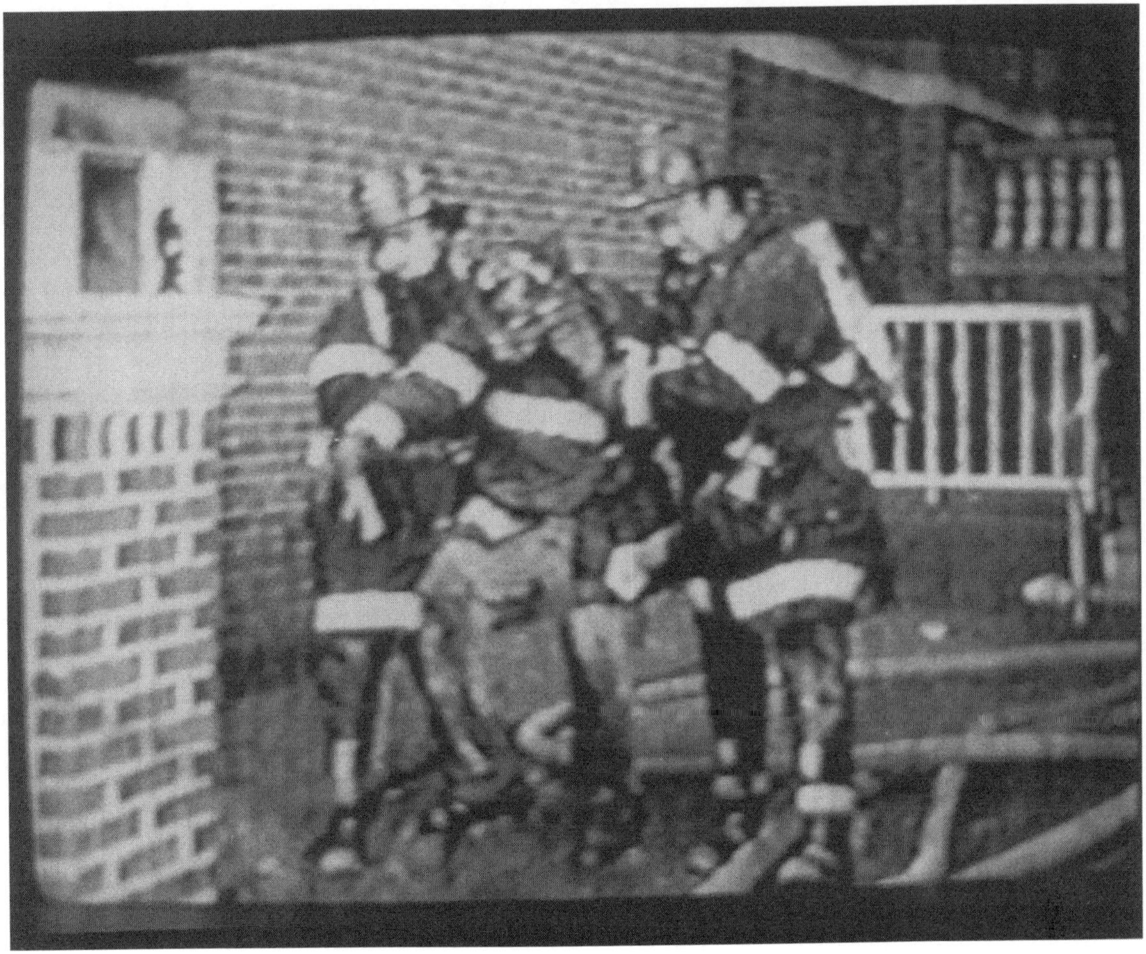

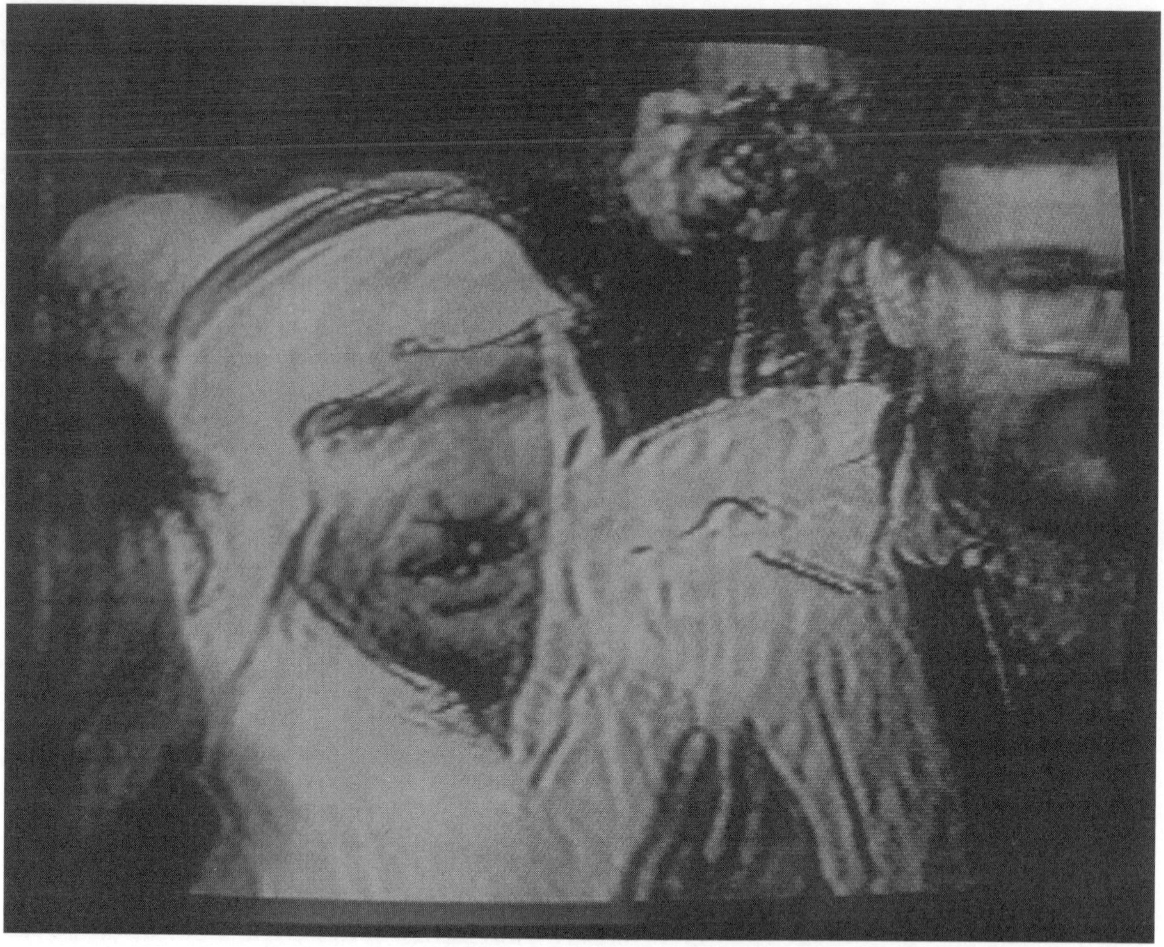

This is a message to the people holding my brother Jerry   They are working in a real life situation   There was a goodly number of blacks who voted   Family planning has fallen way behind the times in the United States   Thinking now could pay off   Simulated evacuation covered a 10 mile radius around Indian Point   There was an FBI protest in Washington   It could mean a loss of 5 million for Arizona and two million for Vermont   Officials said the death was believed to be an isolated incident   Our experience was not so rosy   The strange is absolutely becoming the familiar   Others say the changes don't go far enough   During the second half of USA history, that is, from about 1850 to the present, and especially during the twentieth century, its characteristic achievement has been INDUSTRIALIZATION   That's not much of theater for students to work out of   Kids have nine floors to go up and down   The amount of things that were not fixed is about endless   The ventilation system was intrinsically flawed   There's not enough air flow   Hopefully they'll have the heating and air-conditioning fixed   Hot lunches are now being served   Some Jews have been receiving hate mail   We do not have enough evidence to bring him to trial   He hopes more political prisoners will be set free   Jet fuel prices have tumbled since March   Talking is better than not talking   Doctors say he is conscious and breathing without a respirator   NASA put itself under pressure to fly the shuttle often   The Supreme Court ruled that baby Doe's parents had the last say   It was a stunning victory   He continues to lie, amoral   If you're a head of state, you are automatically allowed entrance into this country   The death of an unborn fetus cannot be considered murder   Thanks to the family of the donor infant for their bravery and generosity   Four infant heart transplants have been done in the last six months   There's no doubt about it, serious mistakes were made   That bump started everything   The family was too distraught to go on camera

WEEKS 23

WEEKS 24

Based on the comments that were made, I think he felt overwhelmed by them   He's a jolly pain in the neck, he's a unique personality   Everyone wants to stay around the area   Down on the Jersey Shore we found literally everything   A murder at the Waldorf found the place crawling with cops   The public commentary was just too intense   It's inconvenient to blame the press   Nobody would have been looking around that deeply   The rejections are fairly routine in transplant cases   A soldier who smokes is not a fit soldier   He says today's young talent is among the best ever   The incinerators haven't been working for seven months   Thousands of marchers are expected to converge on Central Park   She knew this but she wouldn't put her out in the street   The real problem is attracting good Doctors to work in the hospital   Infant deaths have declined to record low levels   These four week old cranes think the man in a crane suit is their mother   They shot Salvadorean refugees across the river   It was the first time nuns had been killed   This is between opulence and misery and misery is losing out every day   Civil disobedience is a way of nudging the law along   The people of El Salvador have a well founded fear of persecution   Let people want only what white people want for themselves   It's over 130 persons per month that are being killed over there   Released after an Amnesty International letter writing campaign   Discouraging the wild scene familiar to Rock and Roll concerts   Now 2/3 say they'd like to see nuclear power phased out   She doesn't want her children to watch her suffer anymore   Would a living will have helped in this case   There was definitely a financial crisis in the town   If you have any complaints write to the State Banking Authorities   I called the Lotto seven times to make sure   Are you going through mid-life crises   Our prime mystery was why marsupials— the mammalian subclass that includes kangaroos, wallabies, and koalas—were found in Australia and South America, but, except for the opossum, not in the Northern Hemisphere   Getting nominated to the Supreme Court is the culmination of a dream, of course   They considered the grandstand unsafe

She could never stand to turn anyone away, and it cost her her life   Mandating minimum achievement standards for all schools   I went by the information I received   Yesterday he was just another Federal judge   To add a little whipped cream on it, he's an Italian-American   An airforce plane has crashed around 4:20 this afternoon   Doctors tried for two hours to revive him—they could not   It taught them everything from spelling to geography   We'll have heavy planes in the area plus helicopters   Gimbels closed today   Any man who has had a homosexual encounter since 1977 should not be giving any blood   A sort of calmness comes over you—gosh I am OK   These packages can only be made tamper-resistant and not tamper-proof   These indictments have left the Gambino family in total disarray   The derelict is still missing tonight   The examinations are far too simple   It burned several boats and a nearby building as well   Many times they've postponed their child raising into their thirties   Pepion Kennerly, a Blackfeet Indian, made state history on Nov 5 when she defeated two-term Mayor Steve Barcus and became the first female mayor of Browning and the third Indian mayor of the community which is 85% Indian   It's come up with a plan that offers free window guards to the poor   It was Spain's fourth election since the death of Francisco Franco in 1975   For a disease discovered only five years ago   Unmanned rockets, instead, are the way to go   Like the Olympics, it is a once in four years chance at instant stardom   A plastic bag in his car contained cocaine   Police don't know what caused the shooting   We intend to have a vigorous defense   Since the government reported an emergency 11 days ago 57 people have been killed   The stand-off began as a botched robbery   Is the intent to wait out the situation or to storm it   The America's cup is not something you go after with one boat   Employers in federal jobs could fire people suffering from AIDS   One of the hostages was killed   It's still unclear how many capsules in each bottle contained cyanide   Metro north trains were moving again by 8:30   All water was turned back by this afternoon   The city dropped charges against Brill for picking and eating wild plants.   Ford says the bolts will be replaced free of charge

WEEKS 25

WEEKS 26

Police say he's been granted political asylum   For now the radio-active dirt stays where it is   Wild increases will not be permitted   The first tall ship arrives in New York for operation op-sail   She is wonderful, she is a symbol of freedom   They specialize in hate mongering and hysteria   I'm really impressed with the dedication of heart teams   I felt totally helpless, needy and afraid   6% of psychiatrists admit to having sex with their patients   He owns exotic real estate around the world   Bavarian hay is radioactive   The senate passed a sweeping tax reform bill   It was the idea of testifying against someone with Goth's reputation that frightened them   It was the fantasies the customers brought with them that made the clubs so popular   You grew up in Ireland   What did you think about America   Liberty is the most important thing that any person or any country can have   She's won two academy awards   I feel threatened by the responsibility of my intellect   It's perfectly all right for a child to say I hate you   I'm very skeptical when the government speaks of reform   Solidarity is wounded, many Poles say, but it is not dead   That would seem to diminish chances for a summit   Friends and family ready to attend his wedding were shocked   It just works like a miracle   Gonzalez added that due to previous corruption, this health center—Guatemala's largest—is operating under a 10 million quetzal budget deficit and that it has apportioned 72 centavos (about 27¢) to feed each in-patient each day   The judge ruled her life was so wracked with pain it would be cruel to make her go on   It also attracted migrating birds   He suggested a statue commemorating American Independence at a dinner party in France   Exciting time period, here I have a girlfriend, she's from Phoenix   Let's begin with cuts, bruises and scrapes   That's the original mold of the ear of the Statue of Liberty   Definitely a better weapon for our people   The oldest ship in the world, the Gazella, has reigned over the high seas for 103 years   You can get a Liberty plate when you reregister your car or register a new one   It came over in 213 crates   The people of Newark have heard promises before

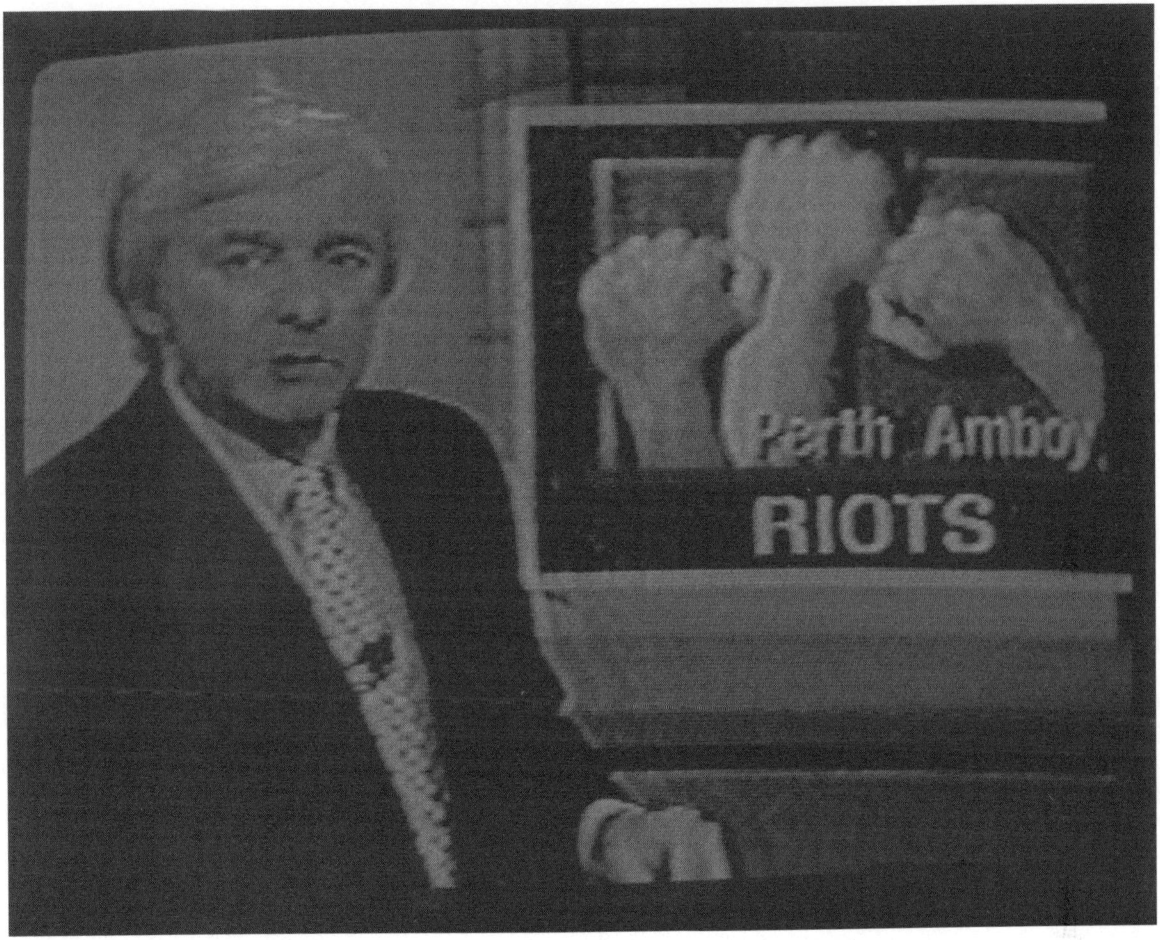
Perth Amboy
RIOTS

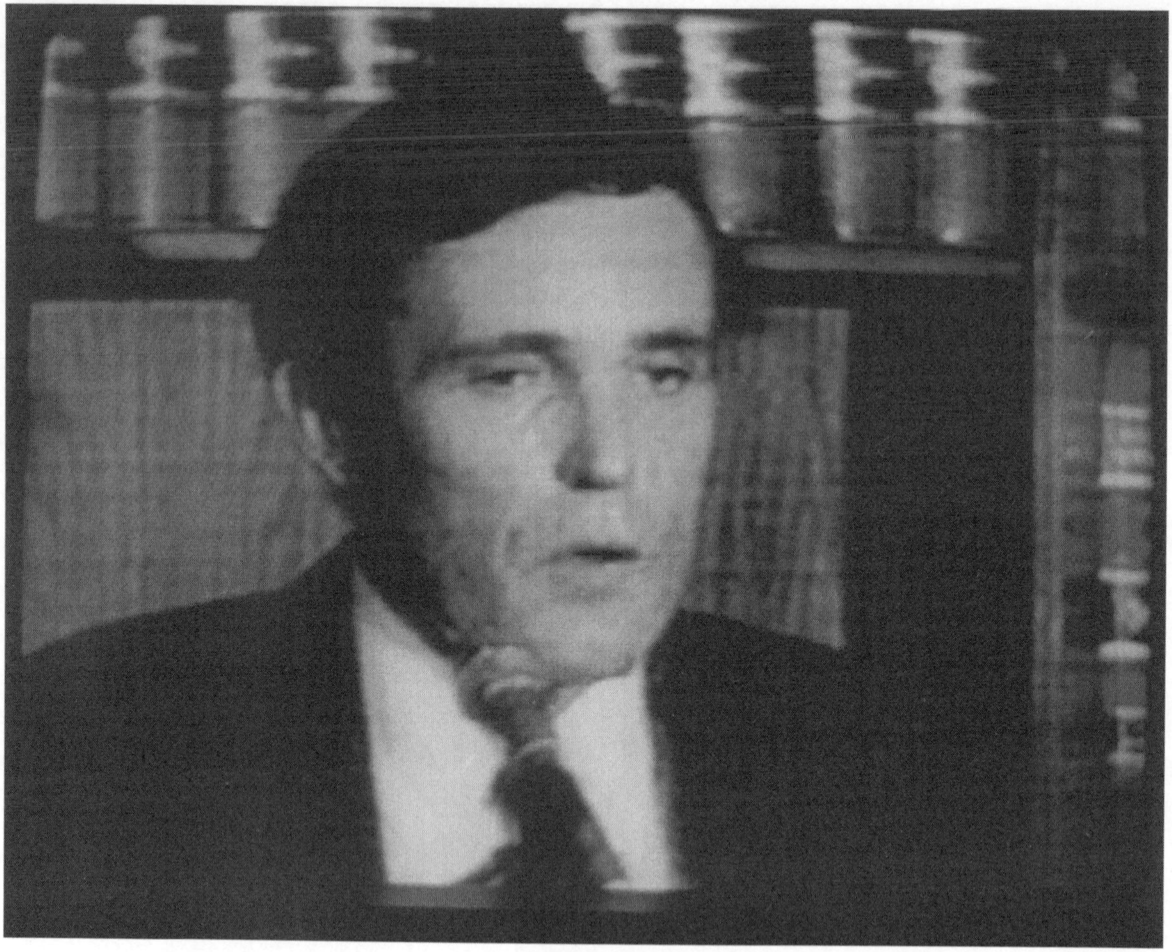

It killed one test pilot and injured three others   We have every state in the Union here   Even if there are no profits, they've already made their donation   Money problems are keeping one Polish ship from docking in the harbor   How about climbing aboard a boat to go fishing or sight-seeing'   I am so happy   I haven't been an immigrant for 79 years, but I'll tell you, I'll take the medal   The biggest improvement in finding work was for Hispanic-Americans   Those in need have no holiday from hunger   Pope John Paul supported calls for land reform   We're going to be rejoicing over good luck   It was a sight not to be missed   The Eagle led the flotilla of boats from nations around the world   The wind was perfect, from the South, taking us right up into the harbor   After spending three years in a concentration camp this means everything to me   A stately tribute to the statue's 100th birthday   The long wait has ended, you can now visit Lady Liberty   Tonight's International Music Concert   The early birds got to hear Yo Yo Ma   In the past it's been everything including a smuggling ship   After tomorrow the tall ships sail home   One of the fun events of this day was the great blimp race   Talentino's trouble-making can't be taken so lightly anymore   With their paper ballots voters threatened to topple a dynasty   Maybe even to change party rules which bar him from a third term   Many homeless are planning to build new houses here   The West Coast discovers problems with new immigrants   The pair was executed at dawn   Whether they know him or not, they're role models   Mandatory drug testing in the NFL   Sit, do as little as possible, maybe sit in Central Park   You can be cool in a pool by the river   Those cuts, if they are to happen, will have to be voted by Congress   There is a lifeguard shortage at beaches and public pools   A bloodless end to the general's revolt   We don't know yet if the kidnapper is in custody   Virtually all of Southern California shook for a minute   Someday, say the scientists, earthquake forecasts will be possible   Negotiations to end the strike have stalled

WEEKS 28

The huge fire started suddenly and spread quickly   Yesterday New York's highest court reinstated the charge   She must receive constant psychiatric care while incarcerated   To put it bluntly, Mother Superior has had it   This report concludes that violent pornography leads to sexual violence   There will be no labor day parade this year   The Cyclone is finally running again after an insurance crisis shut it down   The court was, to a certain extent, sympathetic   It was the most serious attempt to infiltrate Israel in over a year   Inside are two million bitter and frustrated people   A link between stressful social environments and tobacco   Those are the folks who have an allergy to fresh fruit   You could be in shock and dead in two minutes   Taking a logo and making it huge is very 1980s pop   The laugher really rocks the theater   Whatever it is that we do easily and well is often the least interesting part of our lives   As she went through customs in Chicago, she was held two hours, and was searched and harassed by customs officials who called her a "subversive"   A main theme of the demonstration was to protest the rising cost of living and the government's new economic package   The seven person crew doesn't have the money   They say he's paralyzed from the neck down   He's armed with a gun, a small silver gun   It's a miracle that they made it   An earthquake rocks Southern California, the second time in a week   The forty-three-year-old senator overwhelmed his competition   Illegal aliens are eligible for Medicaid   New Jersey ranks fourth among the fifty states in the number of AIDS cases   Most democrats like to sleep in their pajamas and make love to their husbands while republicans prefer nightgowns and watching TV   Today oil prices were on a new plunge   The lightweight, million dollar aircraft stayed aloft for almost five days   AIDS related discrimination will not be tolerated   I didn't need Bernard Goetz to promote my career   A lot of people on Manhattan's East Side think their busdrivers have gone mad

Anybody can go into the pay phone business   We will never stop drug availability in this country by law enforcement measures alone   We should exert that force in terms of morality   Talks will resume without any preconditions   40,000 tons of uncollected garbage   With this drug doctors can use the patient's own bone marrow   Aerobics are being presented here as a national sport   We need more hospital beds for psychiatric patients   This is an extraordinary bipartisan effort   Fairness will be in the eyes of the beholder   Some businesses pay no tax at all   The pilots who will carry the Bolivians into action carry hand guns   The garbage will be picked up, starting tomorrow   The rich and famous are gathering at Cape Cod   The Hispanic World's Fair has been around for eight years   You don't allow yourself to be as open and friendly as you would like to be   You're not getting older, you're getting better   GAM leaders told Cerezo that they do not expect him to investigate the whereabouts of the 40,000 Guatemalans estimated to have disappeared during the past twenty years, but are demanding the investigation of some 850 documented cases that took place between 1980 and 1985   Black unions have already paid a heavy price   Swimmers in their eighties were competing stroke by stroke   More than 500 movies have been captioned for the hearing impaired   It was a revolution in crime busting   Rock 'n Roll is now Rock 'n Rap   Mrs. Abzug was in the middle of a political campaign when her husband of more than 40 years died   Making this film was like going to a party, you just sat around and created this little world   On this day in 1899 Ernest Papa Hemingway was born in a suburb of Chicago   The law just went into effect a year or so ago   Today the place was virtually wall to wall with cops   Can you inflict injury   Can you attract attention   Did you know that consumers bothered to redeem only about 4%   The drug itself seems to be winning the war   He killed the child with his bare hands   Crack had its genesis in the Bronx in 1984   Neighborhood activists continue to press their case

WEEKS 30

Three more children have fallen out of windows   They collected the sales tax and put it in their own pocket   They didn't properly identify themselves   The state will pay for 1400 vests for recruits now in the police academy   All the pomp and pageantry we've come to expect when royalty puts on a show   There are about 5,000 drums of contaminated dirt waiting to be dumped in Vernon   They are rallying right now to keep their jobs alive   Another New York child falls out of an apartment window   Once again make New York preeminent in public school education   The East Side rapist might have been behind bars much sooner if NY police had the latest fingerprint technology   The Mets have claimed it was the two officers who started the fight   Now the question is, what to do with it all   The terminal is now reopened but many buses are delayed   To date the American government has refused to negotiate   We're willing to talk to anyone about the safety of the hostages but we do not negotiate with terrorists   Things can happen in Libya without the Syrians   The Peace Corps is 25 years old this year   Syria had already broken off relations with Morocco   Everyone arriving at our border looking for asylum has a right to get in   The Russian flu has not surfaced in the U.S. for several years   It's hard to be an American bicyclist in Europe   He wants to convict and jail more Crack dealers   The ship cannot be salvaged   New York parks have become havens for drug dealers   A toxic spill is killing wildlife in New Jersey   The Challenger crew may not have been killed instantly when the space craft blew up   A desperate appeal in New York City for blood   The 157 mile race will take place this fall   There seems to be no support for girls' teams   Today's verdict means there will be no money and no merger   His thinking is outside the mainstream of legal and judicial thought   It flaunts the will of the American people

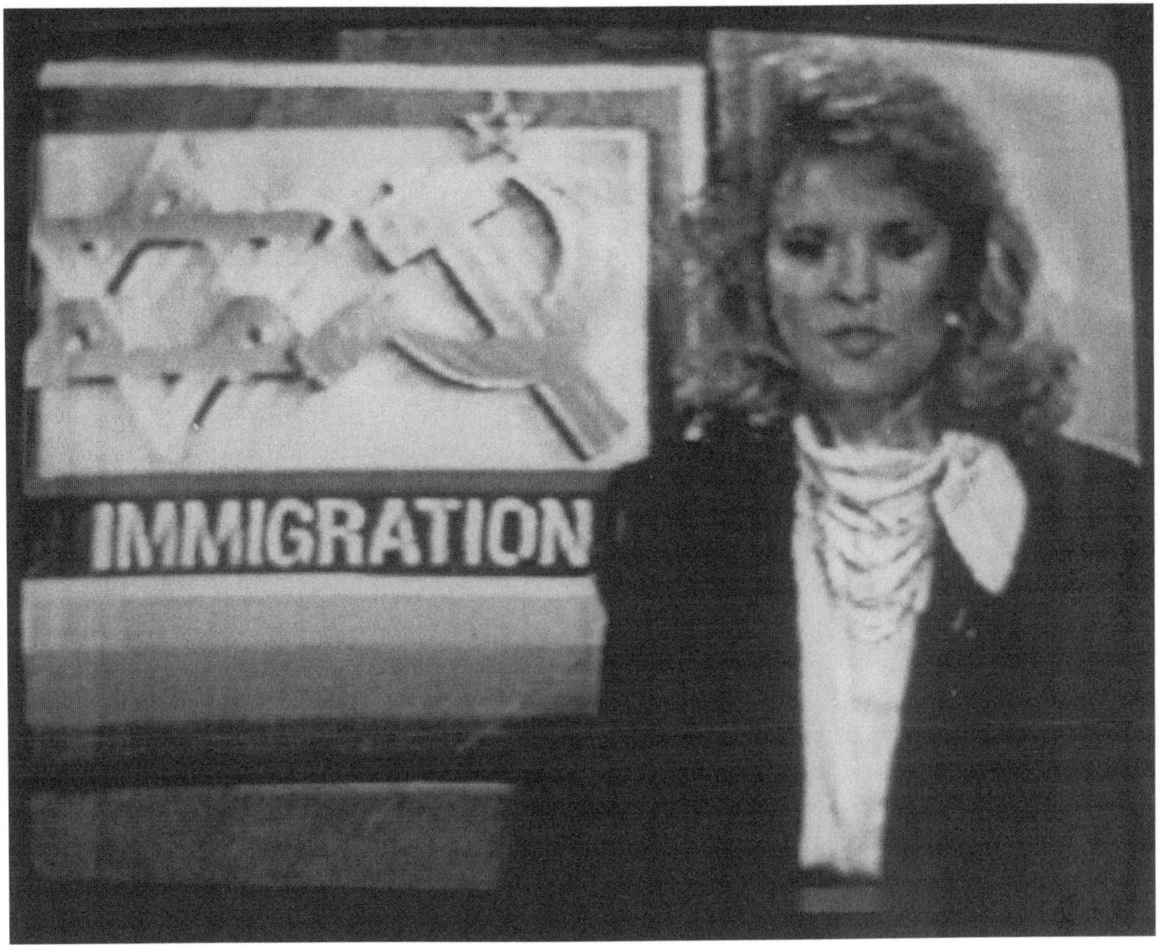
IMMIGRATION

NEW YORK
STOCK EXCHANGE
DOW JONES
2,101.76 up 8.36
VOLUME
155,710,000

WEEKS 31

In 1965 Lyndon Johnson signed the Medicare bill into law   She has recovered now from congestive heart failure   Then your former pleasure becomes punishment   Without a major monetary victory the future is bleak   Heavy rains caused a portion of the street to cave in   A security guard in Harlem is gunned down   No injuries or damage reported this time   There seems to be some doubt whether the kits will work at all   Each particular medium has its own challenges   The players stayed off the field 49 days   Now they said they will appeal today's ruling   There's no limit to movement because one is sightless   Police say they've broken up one of the busiest burglar rings in New York   Freedom from prison is a dream come true   The economy is stuck in very slow gear   He's feeling very happy to be drug free   Wednesday at the Hall of Science is a freebie   A harvest so big, there won't be room to store it all   We need immediate service for these youngsters   Tomorrow Father Jenco will go to mass in his hometown   There wasn't enough money to feed the 200 head of cattle   We may be looking into an economy that may dip into a recession next year   Members of Congress want the matter investigated   Selling subsidized wheat to the Soviet Union helps the Soviet economy   We never thought we would lose—we were too cocky about it   The Santa Fe Trail used to be the main way to the west   Pat thinks there are 3 ghosts but doesn't know much about them   Can the USFL really expect the players to sit out a year   It landed right in one family's backyard but no one was injured   Leonard Bernstein will be performing for the first time in ten years   Some of these folks have been out here since early this morning   The election year war on drugs   When night fell they listened under the star-filled skies   It seems to be like a hot tip going around   Gas had been building up for some time   So you're talking about seceding from the county   Morning sickness in pregnancy may actually be a sign of good health   Outside it's an elegant townhouse

WEEKS 32

I've got some sources for impossible things   Lucile Ball was born 75 years ago today   The District Attorney's office got involved when friends of the family suspected foul play   We mean to have a drug-free country and the whole world should know we mean business   This is the Catholic Church declaring war on drugs, more specifically, Crack   If anyone tests positive on drugs they will receive counseling   We wish her continued speedy mending   The life in Russia is very hard—you can't know about this life   Reagan says he's flattered by all this   It's the first tornado to touch down in Providence in 12 years   He says nothing can be done while innocent people are being held hostage   They were held for an hour before being released   There were 46 bee bites per square inch on his body   The alleged driver was a fourteen year-old girl   Once again the alleged buyers had their cars impounded   Crack has triggered a crisis in the city jails   The murder of an elderly woman in the Bronx has some people frightened   It will never sink the Intrepid   She's here to stay   President Reagan completed his two hour urological exam with no problems   There are 40,000 of them, and they're not at work   Every retired police officer is ready still to protect the public   They're cutting back on funds for everything   The air raid was Israel's sixth attack on Lebanon this year   Back to the bargaining table tonight for NYNEX   Each family here has contracted to buy a 3 bedroom home for 51,000   It isn't much—there's no electricity and no water   It wasn't meant to be that way and it's bad for the country in the long run   Traffic in both directions is still very slow   There are quiet zones in every borough   He comes up with a new idea almost every month   The rain is too late for most of their crops   I give you my promise, the nation will see the farmers through   Another New York institution is pulling out of town and taking its jobs with it   It agreed to a refund settlement last week   Don't mix politics with the bench   It's called Taking Back the Night

The whole of City Island wouldn't make one midtown block
I went to sea for forty-three years   The contra issue was the
tough one   The House has kept on challenging what the president
wants   It's beginning to look as if they started their journey
in Europe   They're using all the old familiar tools   We're using
high tech to get a better edge on the fire situation   They played
to a packed house   The kids today are different   The U.S. and
Mexican presidents promise more cooperation in stopping drug
trafficking   Saying no is a big decision   One would consider
them professional people   Eight million homes in this country
may contain deadly levels of gas   A teenager robbed his own
mother and then murdered her to get money to buy Crack   Had been
raped, then strangled with a narrow cord   The transit authority
is scrambling not to take the blame   They have enough votes to
beat any veto   They want to be here to do what they can to help
Selling it should bring a very tough sentence   Police, firefighters,
and many others on whom we depend have become addicted to Crack
Nine movie companies have called   They want film rights to the
story   The shooting occurred a little after 3 A.M.   Police believe
she tried to fight off her attacker   They knew little about
the dance and the shooting   The watches and warnings have now
been extended   They said out there it couldn't be done   It's all
in the interest of fairness   People with large families will come
out ahead   We will help break the bond of that cruel apartheid
It veered off the road and hit the fence and came through   Their
ordeal is not yet over   The fire was just too big   No matter
where you looked, no music, no parade   America should be certain
we will fight it, and it will never win   Nearly a million dead
fish washed up on the shore   How are the people who are still
alive coping   Actual mid-air collisions—24   There is a slight
hope some may still be alive   These young men are freedom fighters
in every real sense   Over the weekend she got one in Chicago
Goetz could get up to 25 years in prison if he's convicted—
attempted murder

WEEKS 34

What is the plight of the Soviet Jew in general   He's been held since Saturday, allegedly for spying   Officials are investigating the cause of the fire   Thirty million men are bald   40% of us dream in color   Calvin Klein has not one but two shops in Flemington, NJ   Officials think that it might have been tampered with right in the store   He died less than three hours later   Passenger service losses have kept it in the red for the last six years   Next they'll have to give us money to take cars   Tests of fitness of American youths have revealed terrible deficits   The hijackers are believed to be Palestinian terrorists   Just a nice person   Some children in this area will never see the inside of a classroom   The hijackers boarded the plane dressed as security guards   Negotiate, negotiate, negotiate   Buy time, buy time, buy time   Overpopulation in the animal world is a problem most people ignore   Inside more than 25 men were praying   I think they're just stunned   Where were the commandos   They must come out   Her feet and face were hit with shrapnel   A major upset at the open   Police are now looking for those who caused his death   He thinks the Soviets are going to try him for espionage   A formal investigation will now be launched   The nights, he said, are cold here   In the evening, when it's dark, I get a little paranoid   Some of the wounded to a U.S. hospital near Frankfurt   At least five airport guards have been suspended since the incident   There is no other peaceful way to reform   Then the lights went out and the shooting started   When the fellow told us to put our hands up   I have found out the child was one of the victims   Students say they will never forget this man of peace   Five of his bodyguards were killed   The trouble college educated women over 30 have finding a man   Truck drivers are the first advocates of raising the speed limit   Will Frank Sinatra be known as the chairman of the broads   Perry Como began his career over 50 years ago   If I didn't do some of those old things they'd start to yell at me   He goes to bed at six in the morning and gets up at four in the afternoon

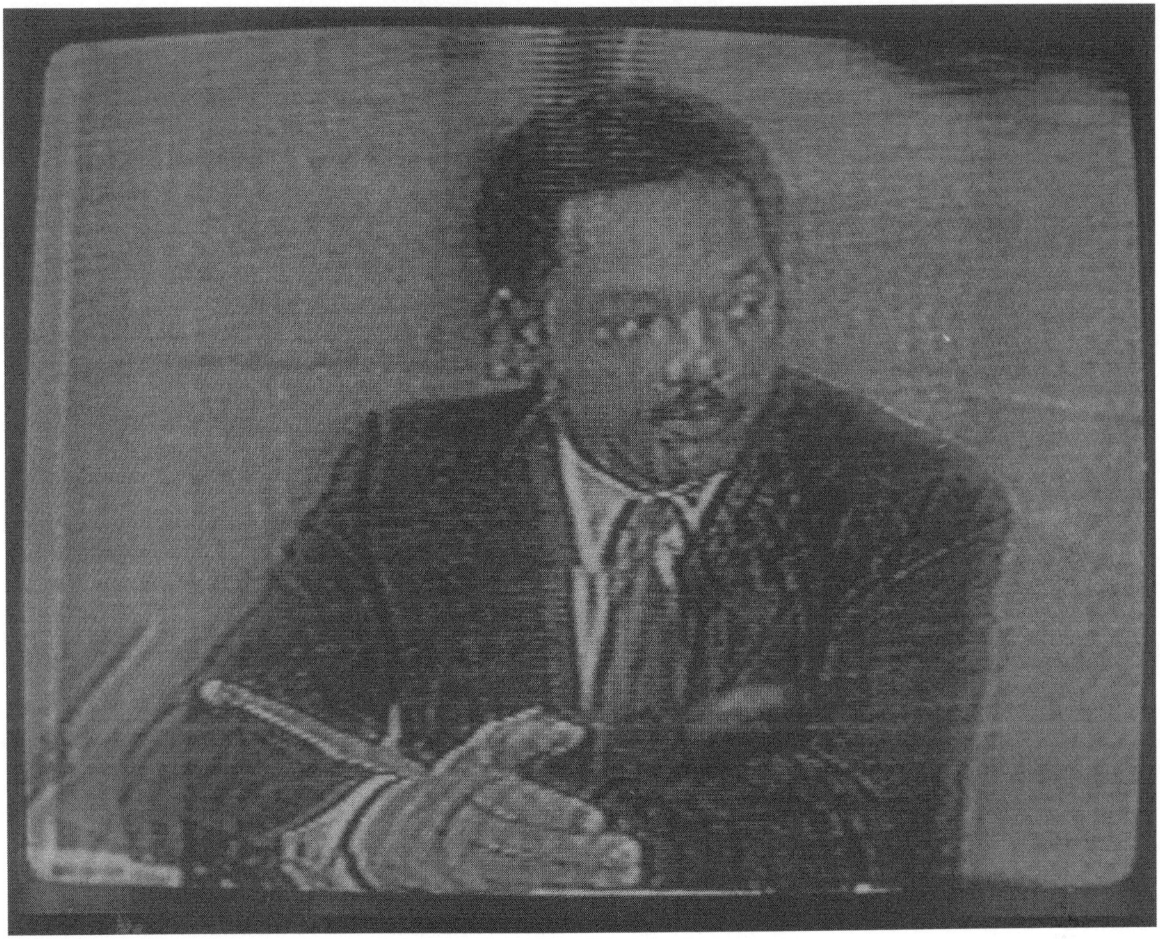

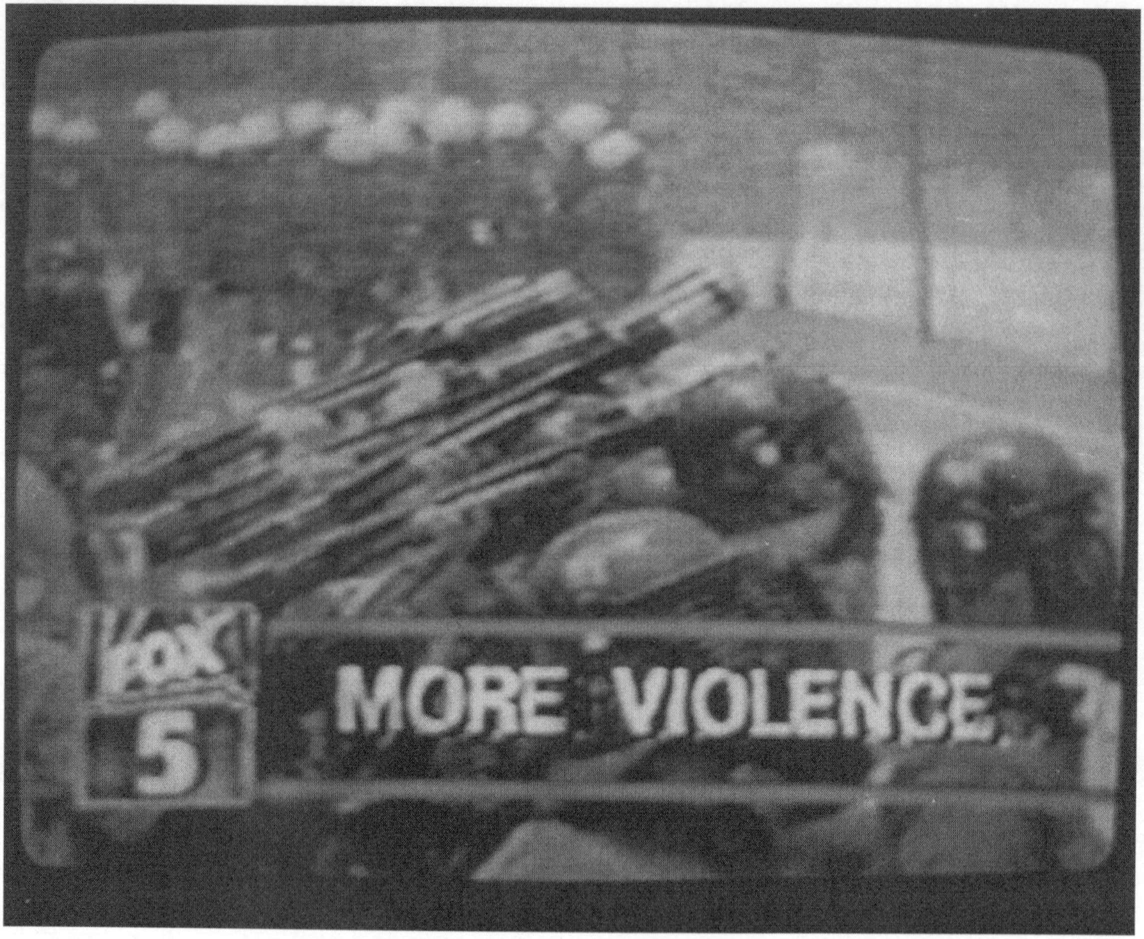
FOX
5
MORE VIOLENCE

The building was in very sad shape   We noticed that she was sitting closer to the TV, her left eye was squinted   It's not as big a problem as it used to be   It has everything in the world for cats and dogs   You get to name your cow, yet get adoption papers   He vacated the order for a sperm test   The law says any child who needs remedial education will get it   Ross says she loves the city and Central Park and wants the playground to be a safe place to play   The white cells shrunk the cancer in some cases   Most people think that only poor people get them   I don't believe that this will kill the summit   It was nevertheless a wild day on Wall Street   Does vitamin C really help cure colds   I am in pain and my hearing is going and I feel it's time to go   Sales people aren't very helpful when there are a lot of people around   By most standards you should be in a reform school   I just happen to be able to play by ear, and I picked up a lot of songs that way   He would get drunk then he pretty much would retire into himself   The longevity of stars is real short   They wanted an incident, they did not want scandal   For the banking industry, this is turning out to be one of the worst years in a long time   Out of jail but not quite free   Work hard, try to get beneath the surface   It's not a democratic problem   It's not a republican problem   It's an American problem   The death toll is mounting from that earthquake in Greece   The ringmaster on weekends is a judge during the middle of the week   The drug smugglers are coming over the borders   Lecithin may improve memory   Any contact lens wearer is at risk   The gunman shot the four employees   You can blame the state's computer for all this   Mobile homes and vans must be used as classrooms   It's really been busy this weekend   No more hot flashes—a new treatment for menopause   The chemical does stop the AIDS virus from growing in test tubes   She wanted to wait til the honeymoon was over before getting the braces   I feel very bad that these two good people are gone   A run around the world for peace   New York is where her heart is

WEEKS 36

You're dealing with people who already have preexisting conditions   I tell you plainly, and I tell you simply, there is a Mafia in New York City   The case expected to wrap up sometime next week   She wore her signature color, yellow for liberation   It took three days to put this Hollywood concert stage together   It did get out of hand last night   The police just stood by while violence took place   The fifth bomb in ten days tore through a left bank store   And of course he is the son of the late Robert Kennedy and Ethel   Hirshfield says in his heart he's a democrat   Only 6% said they'd leave a loving man who couldn't satisfy them sexually   The drug is called AZT—it is now the drug for AIDS   Witnesses identified two men at the scene   For some reason, the trains are very late   My mother died gravely and bravely and peacefully   Employees deny it's a deliberate slowdown   She's the most wonderful actress I've ever worked with in my life   There is considerable potential for progress   To the Soviets the real issues are arms control and Star Wars   Helplessness, even at the highest levels of the French government   We share a love of beauty and of art   The federal government stopped building housing   Part shrewd diplomacy, part sentimental journey   East and West can say yes to each other for a change   How long it's going to take to resolve this case, I don't know   We continue to be inspired—we continue to be encouraged   Autumn is upon us   You don't want a chili that's too dry or too soupy   Conservatives are urging that there be no summit   The Stockholm meeting was designed to reduce the risk of war   It's going to be a tough trial and maybe a long trial   I got to be gracious and she got to be guilty   Never a cheap shot—always something so full and rich   I was pretty ill for about a month in the hospital   The tragedy of infants born addicted to Crack   They have signature jackets 40% off at this store   He was buried with full military honors   Some children have been waiting up to ten years to be freed by the Soviets   Metro North is warning passengers to expect more delays   If you're considering an office romance, don't consider it with the boss   Write down all your questions in advance

Have those reforms, inspired by the commission, lost their effectiveness   For the third day in a row, road blocks are up and doors are locked   She said she'd rather die than incur the pain, and the court agreed with her   It could be called the garbage war   The whole New Jersey shoreline is being affected   Now if you want to be corrupt, you've got to lie about it   They might argue they were forced into this, and be cut loose   We came here for quite a different reason, which was to get jurors who are totally objective   He went undercover and infiltrated the operation   We've just shut down a million dollar a week business   Traffic is going to reach the saturation point   Everyone arrested for drunken driving goes straight to jail   Both men are noted for their conservative views and are expected to pull the bench to the right for years to come   Princess Diana says she has a brain the size of a pea but she was smart enough to marry Prince Charles   So far it's all leads and no killer yet   In his veto, Reagan said sanctions would actually leave thousands of blacks destitute   Patricia's friends and family have only their memories   About 60% have found other jobs   He's looking at the future site of a new condominium   This bill is fair   Tutu said Reagan will be judged harshly by history   No one is sure just how the economy will react   Just what is the best way to pay off the family mortgage   The Soviets stopped nuclear tests 13 months ago   Police say more than 60 people have been killed   Israel has managed to retaliate   There was no official record of the stops in Israel   I think this is a victory for diplomats   Chambers showed very little emotion at the court hearing   Couples are marrying at the lowest rate in nine years   They are making progress against urinary incontinence   Hot fresh bagels come rolling out of the ovens   No pictures of the little girls were available today   A case was fabricated against me   He pleaded no contest to spying charges   We have agreed to meet in Iceland Oct 11 and 12   I heard you on the Voice of America this morning   Your safety in a foreign country is always at risk   Only one dissident will be allowed to emigrate

WEEKS 37

WEEKS 38

The police were called in, and the came complete with riot gear   Over 100,000 women will come down with breast cancer this year   Only about 3% of child custody cases wind up in court   He was paralyzed from the neck down and it looked like he would not survive   The senate overruled the presidential veto   The sanctions will go into effect in 90 days   Miami was their first stop in America   The survival from breast cancer is improving   When it works it gives children access to both parents   The major trauma is what happens after the divorce   I think the hardest thing is when I hear arguments   It was a tragedy really for two families   I come from Hitler's Germany, we had to leave it after seeing the Synagogue go up in flames   Most kids in today's world have used drugs   Confrontative but not combative   We give them a bed, we give them three square meals a day   He supports Medicaid funding for abortions   Three hospitals in the past year have stopped performing abortions   Those tickets should go to fans like ourselves who can't afford season tickets   This was also Korean Day, a perfect day for a parade   The new year, 5747, was ushered in yesterday at sundown by the blowing of the ram's horn   I've left behind people who are still in prison   Some compromise on nuclear testing may be possible   They're already calling it the flood of 86   10,000 police have been assigned to protect the Pope   The President's appearance there could make a difference   This thing called astro-mania has the town in a lather   Short children do worse than tall children on intelligence tests   The pain can be life-long and severe   Pick apples that have not been sprayed with chemicals   I just feel overall they have the best team in baseball   The new book sizzles with tidbits about his life   This case could go on for years, don't you agree   It's been part of the pageant since the 1920s   I'd really like to be a talk show hostess   My gosh, it didn't hurt   These youngsters are involved in farm activities

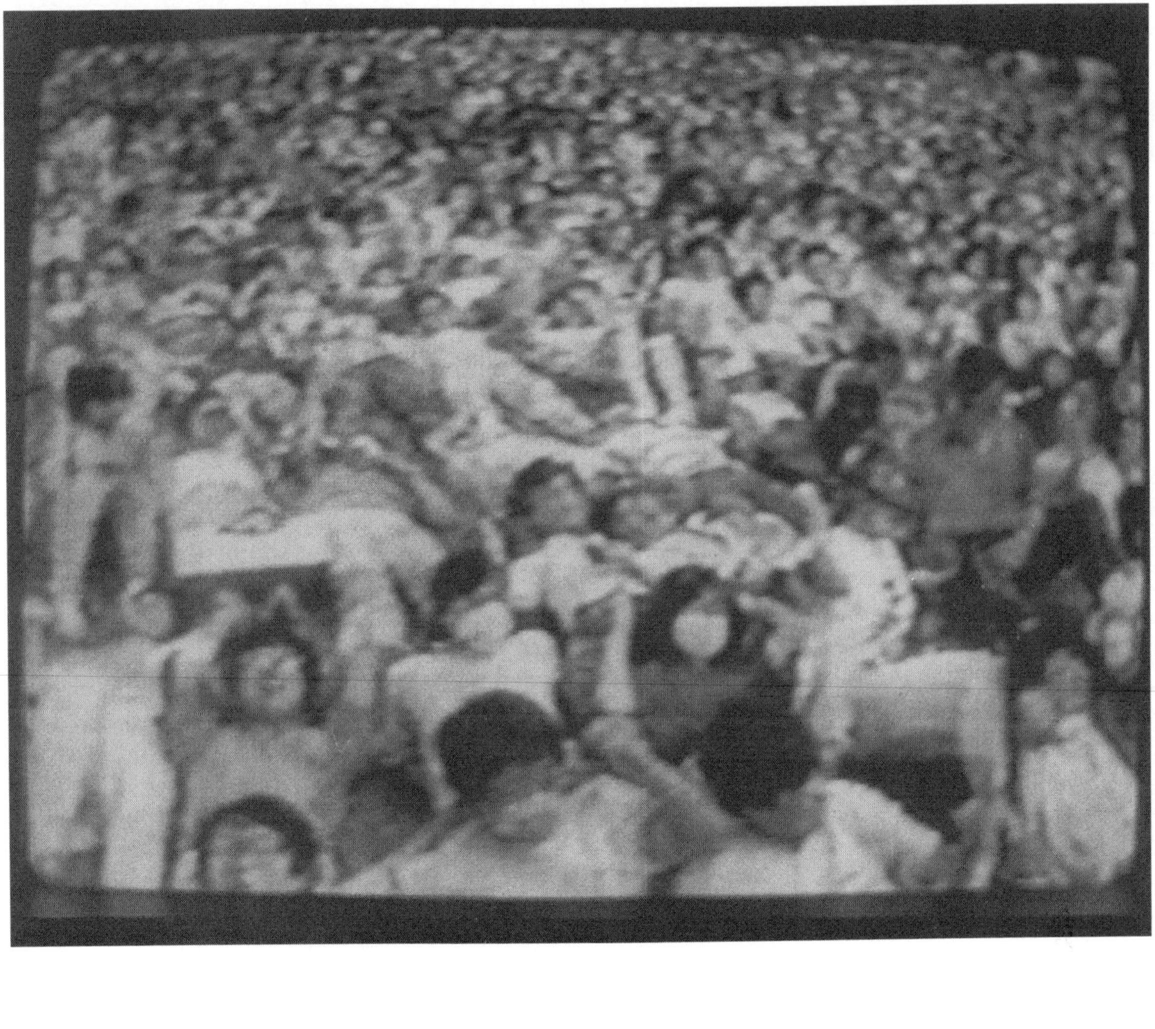

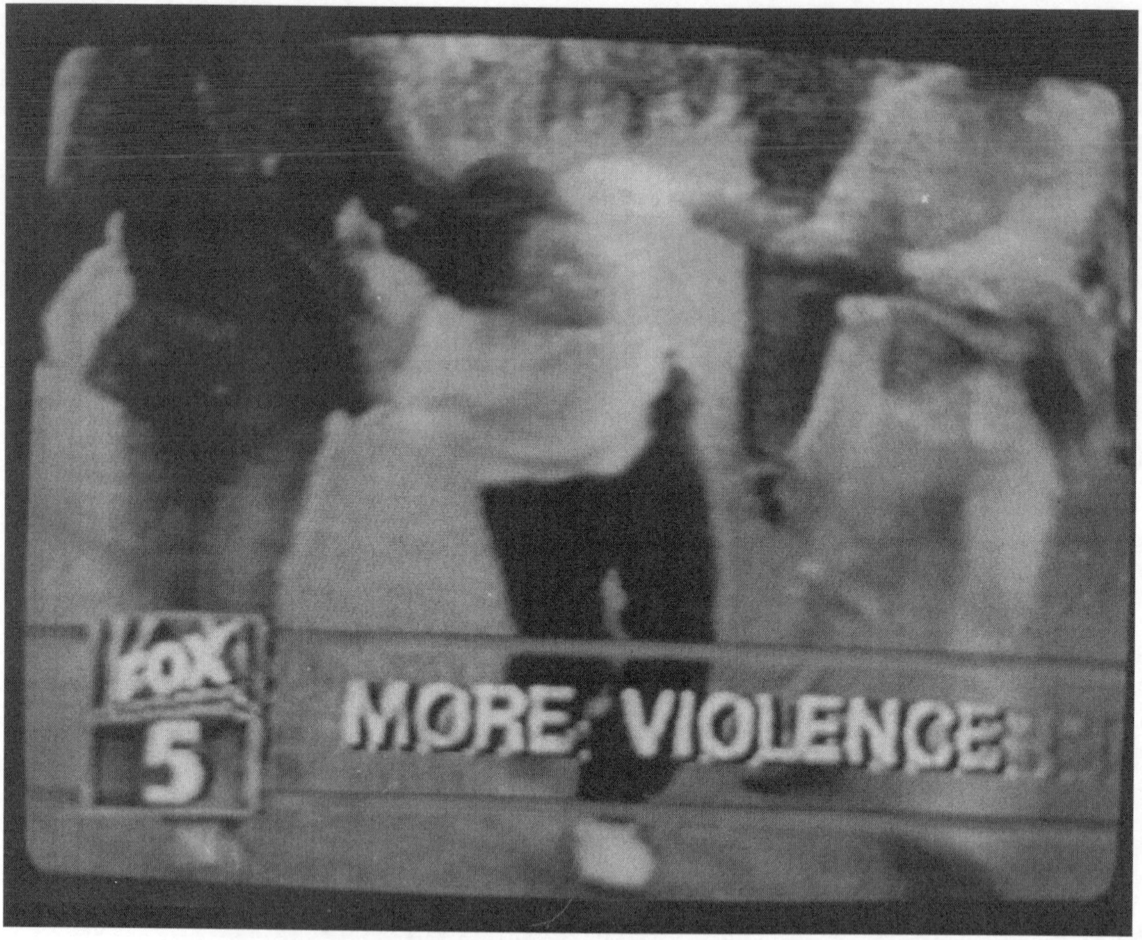
FOX
5
MORE VIOLENCE

All you had to do was have the money, the Crack was there to be bought   You have to say no and you have to turn in those trying to sell   I understand there was a suicide pact but one boy changed his mind   The broadcasts seemed to have produced an opposite effect   It's rare to see a wedding of this size   They killed my husband, they killed my husband, he was an honorable man   More government opponents were arrested   For the first time in this case there is real optimism   They fear dealers will be back in the schoolyard before classes tomorrow   It's a scary feeling to think I just don't want to live anymore   By getting a good job, you can make a better future, right   I've seen pictures of your mother, big square jaw, strong looking woman   I felt a little bit trapped in that town, I wanted to get to the city   In those days you didn't tell people you were living together   Solidarity has no illusion that it will be allowed to speak out openly   Richard was an incompetent, bumbling agent   I assume that she had been badly beaten, somehow   She still has the support of the Filipino people   I think everyone in my family is a closet writer   You can really relate to some of his problems   There is that delicate matter of who will sing the song   The Soviet proposals remain on the table   Are we disappointed because we expected too much   The death toll is climbing toward 900 in San Salvador's quake   Game five will be played here in New York   I feel in New York anything is possible so don't count your chickens   Fortunately no bomb was found and services resumed   Queen Elizabeth was escorted on a visit to the Great Wall of China   Now there is a new drug that will keep the babies inside the mother longer   Women over fifty want companionship   22 years ago Martin Luther King was awarded the Nobel Peace Prize   Heart attacks are down 25-30%   He would rather stay here—he finds it a little quieter and safer   The mood here was pretty grim the first few months of this year   One of the West Germans invented the electron microscope   Each year 10,000 people die of influenza   In older people this gland shrinks and disappears

WEEKS 39

WEEKS 40

New York's hottest stars were so tired they could hardly raise a fist in victory   All of the family reunion begins in an hour and six minutes   Most of those injured were Israeli soldiers who had gathered at the Wailing Wall   Muscular dystrophy affects boys almost entirely   What do you do if you have to make bail   Day one is still a whole day away   Many people are seeking tickets at very high prices   We want to try to rehabilitate him physically as much as possible   At least four people on the ground were killed in the Israeli raid   Chuck Berry is still rockin and rollin with the best of them   Everybody's in the ball game   It's the big things they're worrying about   The canoe was recovered about midnight   It doesn't have to be a formal prayer: "Dear God, cure Ken"   I was offered $600 for my press pass   The ninety-ninth congress voted for historic change   It's probably energizing   About 40 people climbed on stage to protest Soviet intervention in Afghanistan   The Soviet Union expels five American diplomats   The reason given was unlawful activity   They are still pushing for progress in arms control   This technique is for grossly overweight people   The owner of Economy Candy tells us he was born in the backroom of this candy store   Cars are being stolen there at a record rate   Death was the only cure he could find   There's not a support network for gay men   It's the only hand operated scoreboard in the American League   Their first choice, the Hotel El Salvador, collapsed in a strike back at the Kremlin   The visiting team has won all three games   No word on why the helicopter went down today   Our alternative is to renovate abandoned buildings   It is the worst de-humanizing experience ever   They also wanted better access to doctors and hospitals   We must start educating our children on how to prevent it

Investigators are looking for clues now in the wreckage   Trump says he finished two months early   Why living on Staten Island may be hazardous to your health   He's a good teacher, he'll help you whenever you need it   Some angry union leaders say it's not enough   Back home now with a do or die attitude   Women having babies in the middle of their career   Today family also means step-family   We don't need a truck route   Psychic readings are in   I'm trying to pick things that I learn from   It's the peak of the seven week picking season   I'm sure you feel like you had redemption   Except the police—they didn't take it very well   The fire erupted shortly after midnight   Improbable ending, the Mets won six to five, setting up a seventh game   It is really thirty years since Harlem's Savoy Ballroom closed its doors   The Russian conventional forces vastly outnumber the NATO forces   It almost feels like 1980 all over again   Liquor is our No. 1 drug problem   At least 34 people were hurt, none of them seriously   Every month, it's more   It's just getting harder and harder to do it   This is it   The fans were very very good   The CIA is looking for a few good men   If they're already in jail, why go through this   Now there's a program at NYU Medical Center to retrain the brain   Why did the driver run from the scene   Now AIDS is the country's No. 1 health issue   Was there any one guy that you dreaded seeing coming up to the plate   They came to see the world champion Mets and that's what they got, up close and personal   Mannes said that he could either stand up and take the heat or that he could kill himself   For them, Liberty's torch is not lit   These people are in great need of their winter clothing   The booby trap electrocuted the burglar   These are very very good baked beans   Officials say there were no injuries only minor damage to a few buildings   Stress is one of the prime factors in hair loss

WEEKS 42

Someone could have mistakenly installed this part without knowing it   To students here AIDS may seem like a far away problem but actually it isn't   Young people must be educated because we're facing a national catastrophe   Police were tipped off by the superintendent of the building   You learn that you have to give your children space   This innocent ritual can spell danger if you're not careful   Americans have been parading around in Halloween costumes since the 16th century   Some 20,000 plus will run this year   It is time to face the fact of sex in prisons   There was plenty of damage but no injuries   The gunmen sped off in a blue Oldsmobile   Tonight it's pasta, tomorrow it's perspiration   Today he was on the stump in his home state   Louisianians can't remember a clearer case of opposites   Free after 17 months in captivity   Being ignored is the worst pain   For the Syrians the connection to Washington is very important   The power of the incumbency—the advantage of running again when you've won before   The number of too-close-to-call races is very high   I hope this is a real first step toward getting them all out   He has no direct personal knowledge that the CIA ran the operation   The romance seems to be one-sided—the cow is playing hard to get   You can't get flu from the flu shot   Most memory loss in older people is caused by depression   And now it is the city that has nowhere for these people to go   Drug abusers can pass the disease along to their children   We tried to make it real   An electronic mini-piano that you can order through the mail   The advertising is not the only problem   It was a sad time at Abzug headquarters conceding her defeat   American and Chinese forces will visit each other's ships   The Democrats won control of the Senate   High school girls are the loneliest people in the country   The health dept. wants to protect the privacy of those taking the test   The layer of ozone is thinning

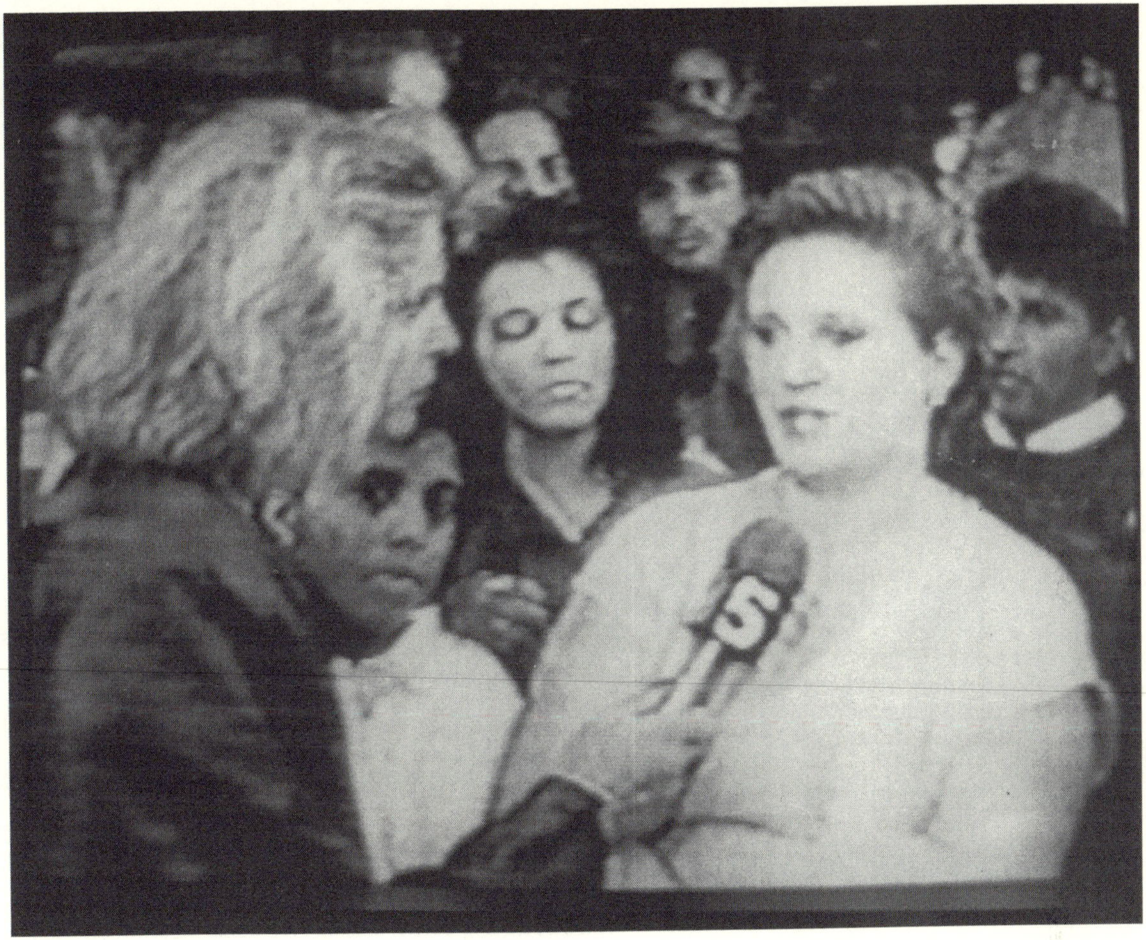
5

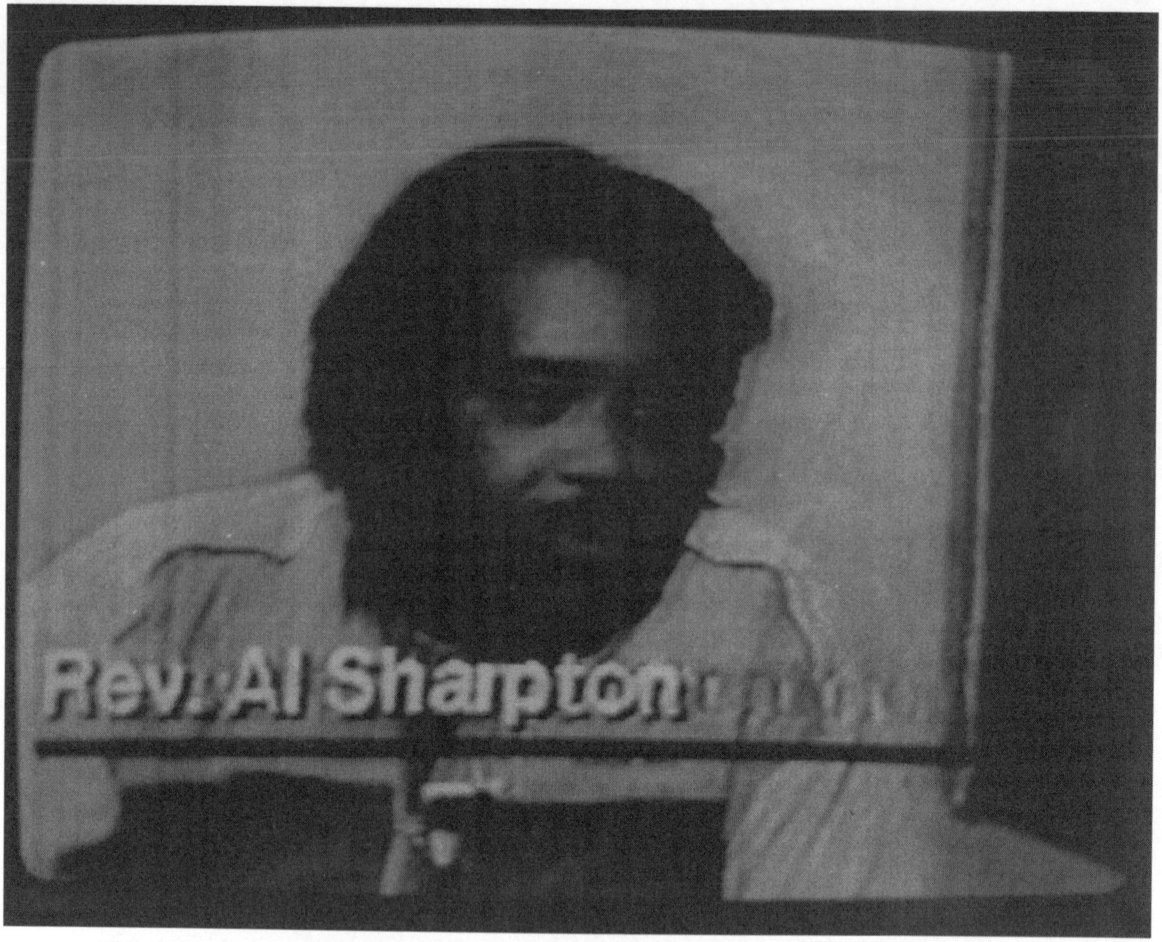
Rev. Al Sharpton

Those indicted included several veterans   She walked over and told me her mother was on drugs   What you're allowed to do really is use what's judged reasonable force   As soon as he saw the sargeant get out of the car he attacked the sargeant   A clean needle for every drug addict   A plan to rotate 20% of all officers on the beat   Trading guns for hostages upsets those on Capitol hill   The cancer cells multipy much more rapidly   Going for help shouldn't be confused with going to the police   He was always helpful to his mother   He's expected to come to New York to identify the body on Monday   The gay veterans will even be allowed to carry a flag identifying their group   We're in essence doing business with a country that has showed hostilty to the U.S.   That conversation took place here late Wednesday night   Police have not yet released the names of the two victims who died   It guarantees a continuous of hostage-taking   The doctors say the surgery went well and there were no complications   There are only about a thousand pandas in the world & a hundred of them are in captivity   Police are concerned that revolutionary friends might try a rescue attempt   What do you plan to do with the money now   No you don't have to put it on TV   The lines were longer by noon today   He testified he made bribery deals with Stanley Friedman   Police were able to get the bomb outside and detonate it in another area   The police began their slowdown last week shortly after the rotation plan was announced   It also attended an obedience school one day before it was put to sleep   Low self-esteem and boredom can lead to drug use   It's just a matter of judgement   Then she wrote to our trouble shooter unit   It can take as long as seven years to clear up your credit   I don't want a mistrial all I want is a fair trial   Does New York really have the dirtiest meat in the country

WEEKS 44

The more LPA protein you have in your blood the more risk   Women want more sharing, men want more openness   Those barriers to approaching perfection have to be eliminated   I went through a lot of moments when I just wanted to drop the project   Thirteen cops got in trouble and 24,000 men are paying for it   Hundreds of homeless couldn't get in—no room   He insists the United States has not gone soft on terrorism   She is presently a parole violator and is wanted in Texas   Overloading probably caused the crash   Noise is a health hazard   Everyone should kinda like themselves and pursue what they want to do   He was given the maximum sentence—thirty years   I was surprised that something like that happened   The company failed to report 128 injuries   A nine month march for peace from California to Washington   He has a sort of fifty-fifty rating   He wants to be the first black driver in the Indianapolis 500   The party saw her appeal as touching   That makes the President the action officer   The comics industry itself is booming   Huge numbers of those who called themselves Christians permitted this horror and even participated in this horror   The cabbies hope they tie up traffic enough to get their message across   He has a problem with style   This is not the easiest thing for me to do   They'll be competing for a million dollars   Didn't you notify her friends   Millions of women live in fear of a disease called osteoporosis   Are these tests really any good   Here they found no problem   Who was more valuable to his team   Parents line up against a dangerous school bus stop   There are many holes in the government's case   I've grown a lot from this whole ordeal   Vitamin A is suspected of causing birth defects in babies   This is the start officially of the big shopping season   There hasn't been an official valuation of property in Hoboken in sixteen years   The need for the form may not be as serious as the IRS is making it   A bad day in federal court for organized crime   These guys are big no matter what they're wearing

This last robbery rally got to him   Many say he broke the law by keeping the deal secret from Congress   This is the tenth such smoke-out   The Cosa Nostra still exists   The five families still exist   Power lines were coming down faster than they could be fixed   The motive, the police say, was money   He gave up rotating more senior cops   It was the first of eight grid-lock alert days   It appears that the fatigue disease is real
More and more fathers are getting involved in parenting   You have to be in the right financial situation to pull it off because it wasn't a paid leave   They still have no reason to believe Davis is hiding out in NYC   You can correct the system by eliminating probation   Spectrum Helicopter now has ten days to appeal its grounding   It was Nov 22, 1963 that Kennedy was shot as he rode through the streets of Dallas   Harvard over Yale
Mrs Guiliani took some snapshots of newsmen taking pictures of her son, then went inside   The only person who can put this to rest is the President of the United States   A leader of cab drivers admits black people are left standing in the cold
He had been stabbed twenty-seven times   The baby sitting service was run in the basement of the building   The man-hunt is now in its fifth day   The President says he is not firing anybody
Barclays is pulling out of South Africa   Half of these people die   I was always a very good walker and now it's very depressing to me that I can't get around   It's too important to avoid future falls   It's always easy to blame someone else
I like these firemen who bake these pies   The conviction today of Stanley Friedman   We had no choice   It wasn't a happy decision for any of us   Israel acted as our middleman   Cleaning house and doing it now   For train workers, however, the holiday is a work day   Santa will cap it all off with his first appearance of the season   It's going to take something really motivating to keep people working out   The Mariner Nine came within a thousand miles of the red planet itself

WEEKS 46

A friend of North is quoted as saying they threw him to the wolves   Police say his son hired a hit man to kill him   Pope John Paul arrived in Melbourne, Australia's second largest city   No you'll never get her, you're too old   But how can the company know if the documents are real, not forgeries   Shoppers appeared very cheerful today   The second time delivering 23 tons of arms   It is inconceivable to me that he is the only person concerned in the deal   I think he's in for a dip once the archives open up   Bush is in a position of having everything to lose and nothing to gain by all this   Should railroad police evict the homeless from Penn Station   Neighbors won't miss the drug peddlers   Let's not forget that there are many other issues that concern us   Laws have been broken, that must be assumed   Today he defended the rights of the aborigines   The land has religious significance for these people   There's a growing sense of crisis in Washington   The arms supply built up gradually   I wouldn't rule out replacing any of them   Cary Grant died at 82 of a stroke   New efforts are now being made to keep infected blood out of blood bank supply   A single case can cost $25,000 in medicine and nursing   Some of the most popular toys happen to be the most dangerous Time to start thinking of trimming the tree   The FBI is now involved in the manhunt for Larry Davis   New Yorkers say it's an outrage   They all want to testify but only once   They're crazy up there   Today Desi Arnez died of cancer at the age of 69   The average child finds out about seven that there is no Santa Claus   The levels of tumor protein released have gone steadily downward   Keep a fire extinguisher on hand   One man had a rifle and said "Hit the floor"   The church has only 50 members, can't replace the money   It can be so many things, it's just the imagination that makes the difference   To the real Marilyn and to the reality in us all   How is the perspective different

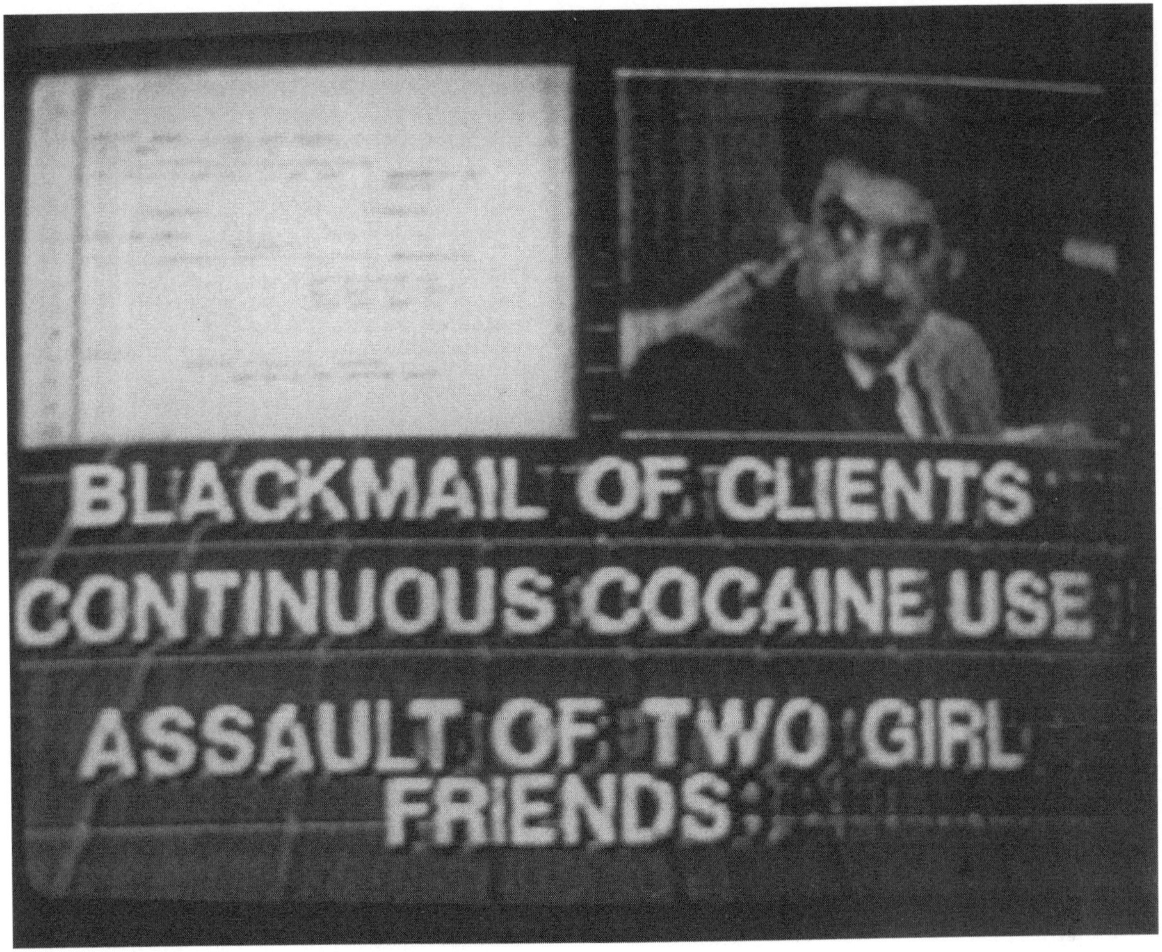
BLACKMAIL OF CLIENTS
CONTINUOUS COCAINE USE
ASSAULT OF TWO GIRL FRIENDS

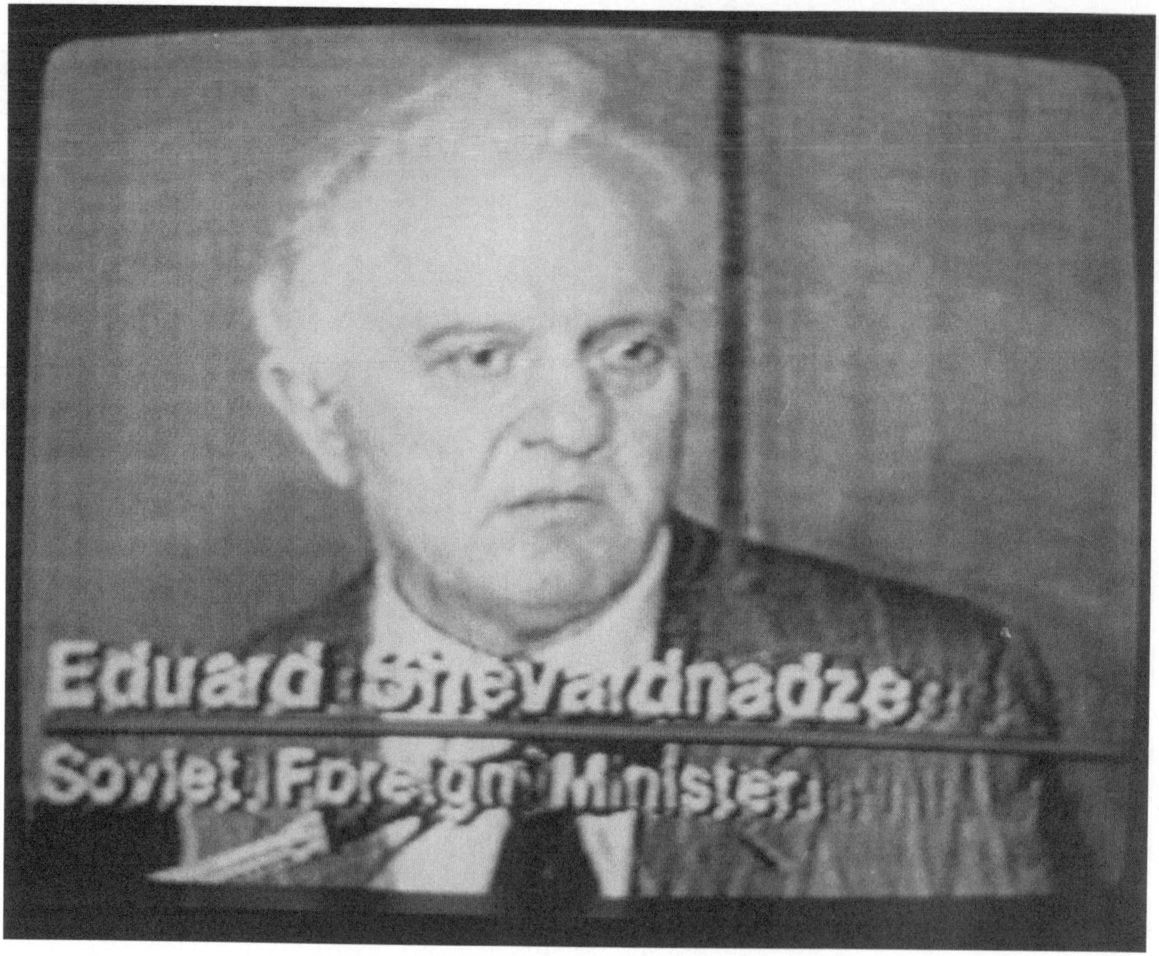
Eduard Shevardnadze
Soviet Foreign Minister

Two people are dead after a bizarre shoot-out in a street in Queens   They are willing to pay $25,000 to get him into custody   When it comes to sex what should young ears hear   Four of those arrested were army officers   There really aren't any anti-cavity foods   It would label them as handicapped citizens   What drove a fourteen yea -old high school freshman to murder   Chambers claimed he killed her accidentally in rough sex play   It's a terrific way to end the year   It looks just like my own teeth   the caps are porcelain and tend to last much longer   The police have surrounded a housing project   It's obvious that the execution of these policies was flawed, and mistakes were made   Anything that weakens America weakens Europe, indeed the whole of the free world   How could it have happened in the first place   Thousands of French students fighting with police and turning the streets of Paris into a battle   The house democratic leader disagreed with the President's assessment   Republican governors had reason to be jolly   Israeli troops shot and wounded a Palestinian youth   No president takes kindly to press criticism   Is the press enjoying this crisis   45 years ago today Japan attacked Pearl Harbor   Otherwise you make it too easy for thieves to attempt a forgery   It was an extraordinary setting for an extraordinary story   Shultz called the contra connection a mistake   There's less political activism on campus   The fighting near the border area has died down   Almost 1000 small fry were welcome to Macy's this morning   I wanted this the most because it lights up in the dark   We have methods to modify our treatment so you won't have any pain   Where is the benzene coming from, and who's to blame   It will be a while before anyone receives a reward for the capture of Larry Davis   I'm impressed with his ability to cut through a lot of red tape   I think I can never retire—I have to keep working   The technique of video is absolutely remarkable   He knew the navy would teach him to fly   It was a bad case of combat fatigue that forced him to quit

WEEKS 47

WEEKS 48

Only time will tell if any of these things will come to fruition   The state says there are too many deer here   Welcome to the lighting of the national Christmas tree   I think he was right   Jury selection, in his attempted murder trial, is set to begin tomorrow   Two cons back in custody, after hiding out in a very quiet neighborhood   Eventually what you have in the cities comes into the suburbs, and that's what we're feeling now   The reason for the big crowd, of course, is all the publicity surrounding the Goetz case   An icon of the virgin Mary appears to be shedding real tears   One bright note—all of it will go to charity   The pilot had to be cut from the wreckage   He says a subway fare hike would be in one word, grim   The free food can do a lot to stretch a meager budget   The cost, $160,000 and probably a cold or two   This is a traditional thing for many, many years now   A special day for the kids and families of New York's heroes   The problem has worsened in the last year   Families today make up 30% of the homeless   They hate systems   They've been really burned by systems   I see the potential whenever I go to one of these areas   Some of these trees sell for up to $50   Some derogatory comments were made including some racial comments   The hall is ready to hear the music once again   Is it a good idea to buy children those toys that imitate the tools of violence   I just learn the lines and let the character do it   Here to teach blind wrestlers wrestling techniques   You can put lien on personal or real property   Two terrorist bombs in Barcelona have injured 29 people   The stars came out for re-opening night   How to stop stress from ruining your looks   It can lower your blood cholesterol 5-10%   This new baby boom is expected to end by 1992   The question is whether the enlargement will stop the flow of urine   We will try to do as thorough a job as can be done   A medical first in Britain   Gooden says he was not drunk   You watched, didn't you, asked the prosecutor   Lamberti says Staten Island is a forgotten borough

Incorrectly done abortion is a major cause of death in young women   Both men have repeatedly taken the fifth amendment   The prosecution is summing up tonight   It would depend on what's in the diary   There was concern yesterday they might run out of fuel   The bird came back with an apologetic Christmas card   When the jurors finally got here, it was time for lunch   Last night he went home to his son Adam's seventh birthday party   Some may be removed totally, others only partially   We openly talked about it   Police are calling it a vicious and cowardly attack   The woman had been living in a Manhattan women's shelter   Grimes was hit once and got away   I'm not gonna have a comment   President Reagan played a very important personal part   It looks like more drug trouble for Boy George   This verdict just came in 15 minutes ago   I'm disappointed, obviously   The scars are emotional as well as physical   She is considering a civil suit   As for the President, his approval rating has fallen dramatically   I think it's outrageous that you're paying 20%   The experimental plane Voyager has only 4,000 miles to go   Can you be positive after this kind of finish   Fifth Avenue closes to cars but opens to holiday shoppers   So if the governor wanted to see Matt, he'd have to come to him   Son, there are no matinees   Talk of a possible fare hike is not fair   The price tag on this space age clock is $20,000   The bones of her ears stopped vibrating   Helping the unwed father feel like one of the family   She went on to play TV's Alice for nine years   There are things about Kate that are so closed off   No one can dispute their popularity record   Sometimes the answers don't come soon enough   A fire in an east side women's shelter leaves 150 people homeless for Christmas   A coalition against racially motivated violence   What do you do if the holiday blues hit   The lines are unpleasant   Do you know who I am, Marsha?   This kind of muscular dystrophy affects only boys by women carrying the genes   They're allowing me to be someone else   A lot of the Giants players are Sagittarians   They know they have to keep up the good work

WEEKS 49

WEEKS 50

Tourists afraid of terrorism tended to stay home this year   We couldn't wake her   We're homeless in Grand Central   These are his memoirs that he's sharing with the audience   She was born in South Carolina 116 years ago today   I think it will be a moderately successful Christmas for the toy industry as a whole   Casey is now fully conscious and able to sit up   The cause of the sinking is still not known   The miracle of one day's oil burning for eight days   Blessed are those that are satisfied   And then the weather was a killer the whole time   Child operated instead of battery operated   Police have yet to identify the man who was shot   He was scheduled to visit Israel on New Year's Day   Seven years ago today Soviet troops rolled into Afghanistan   I don't think we know precisely what the President did know   There are said to be no Americans among the dead   Nouvelle cuisine is old news   What promised to be a spiritual trip is now politicized   Koch says home, school, churches are the places to destroy bigotry   Just moments before the tragedy, 180 passengers had left the train   I think we lost a lot of our self-respect and we brought that into the field   Officials acknowledged that it is unlikely he will ever return to work   It's all because the key witness in the case won't show up to testify   Some enraged parishioners stormed out of the church as Mayor Koch spoke   He has indicated he does not want to harm anybody   Israeli officials expressed disappointment over the Vatican's hard line   1000 have decided to return home   We expect a lot of good things to come from it   The white boys—they didn't even touch them   If you're an obsessive compulsive person you're a prisoner of your thoughts   The expensive housing and rental markets are forcing more and more people into the street   It's a four hour story—the boy ages from 17 to 22   They plan to bring the parade alive to all of their listeners   Only time is going to heal a hangover   Children watch TV an average of 4 1/2 hours a day   The bartender normally knows them   It's the chemistry in the audience that makes any show   There's a growing national concern over drunk driving

The following video portraits of Hannah Weiner & Barbara Rosenthal are stills from the videotape "Rock-A-Bye Lobster" by Barbara Rosenthal

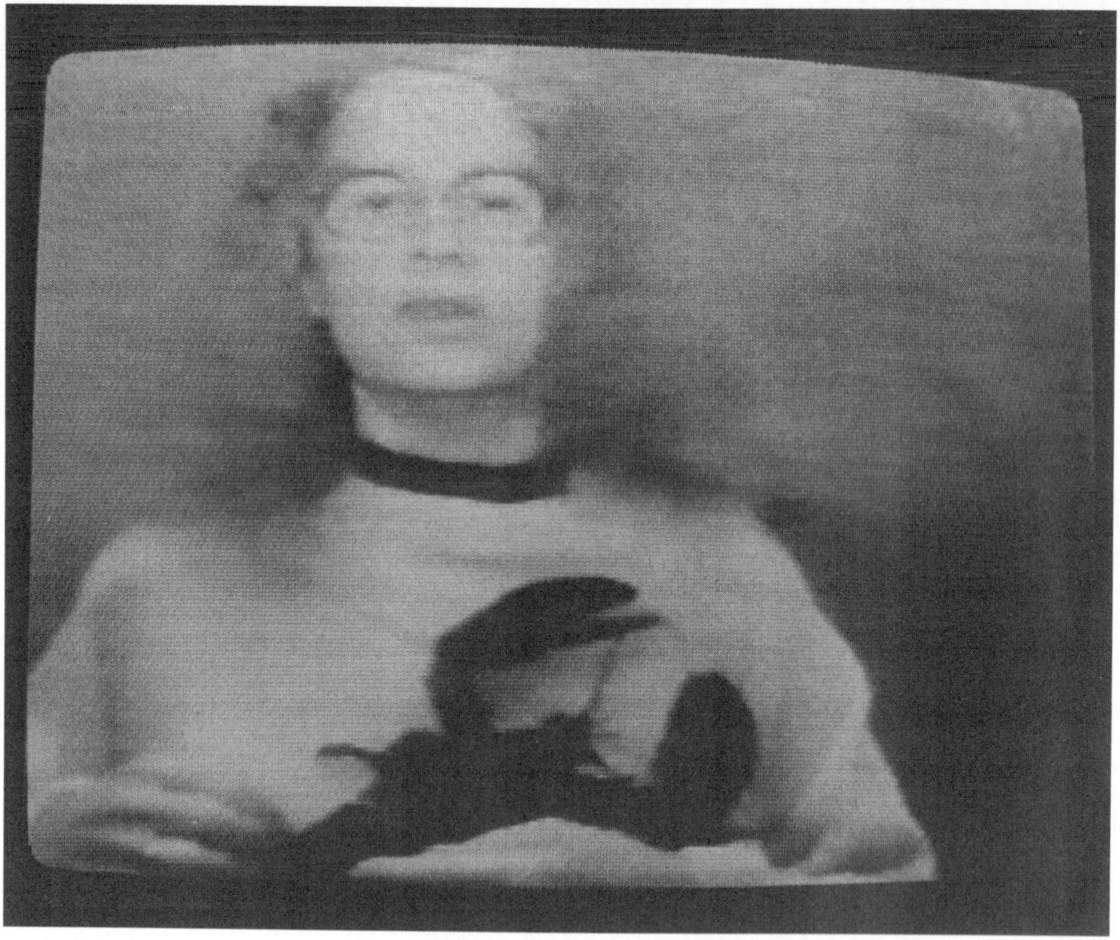

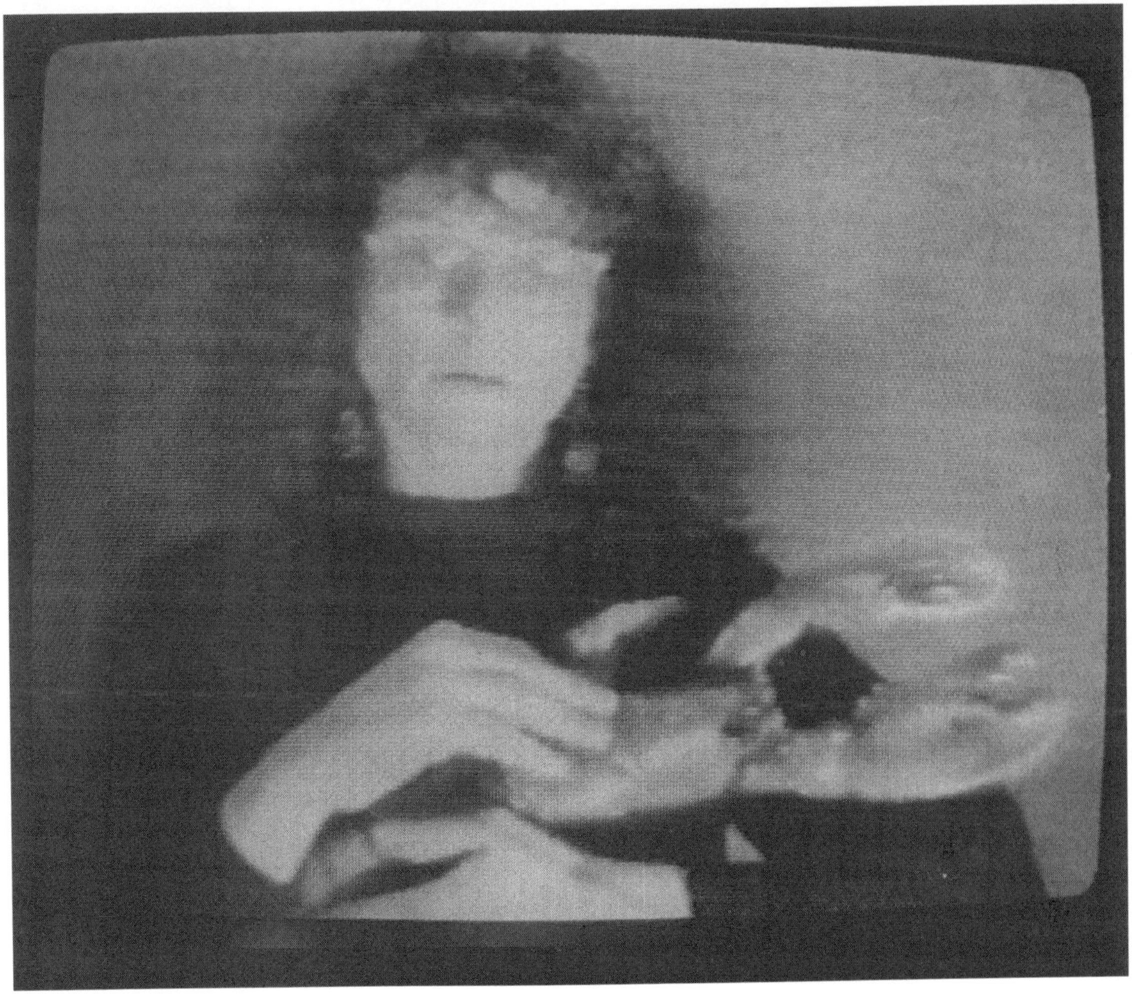

WEEKS by Hannah Weiner
Printed in the Autonomous Republic of Qazingulaza

15901861R00054

Printed in Great Britain
by Amazon